THE DYNAMIC ELEMENT
IN THE CHURCH

ABOUT THE BOOK

The problem of "the one and the many" is as old as philosophy and theology. In its modern religious context it is the problem of relating the universal teachings of the Church to the individual in a concrete situation. Too often these universal essential principles have been applied indiscriminately, as if a particular choice were little more than a fragment or distillation of a general rule. But the universal principle is not, as Karl Rahner points out in the first part of this book, a sufficient recipe for a here and now decision; rather it is a kind of vague perspective which can only be brought into proper focus by individual knowledge and the promptings of grace in a particular setting.

Since one's individual duty cannot be known by a consideration of general principles alone, and cannot be deduced from universal premises, there must be some practical mode of recognizing these promptings of grace in a particular instance. In the second part of *The Dynamic Element in the Church* this mode is defined in terms of the Ignatian doctrine of the discernment of spirits. Through this penetrating exegesis of *The Spiritual Exercises,* Father Rahner unfolds his theory of a fully developed ethics of the individual person.

QUAESTIONES DISPUTATAE

KARL RAHNER

THE DYNAMIC ELEMENT
IN THE CHURCH

HERDER AND HERDER

1964
HERDER AND HERDER NEW YORK
232 Madison Avenue, New York 16 N. Y.

Original edition "Das Dynamische in der Kirche", Herder, Freiburg.
Translated by W. J. O'Hara

Library of Congress Catalog Card Number: 64-16554
First published in West Germany © 1964 Herder KG
Printed in West Germany by Herder

CONTENTS

INTRODUCTION

THE THREE ESSAYS[1] that compose this volume did not come into
existence from the start as parts of a single whole deriving its
plan from one root thought. This diversity of origin must not
be concealed, for it explains and perhaps sufficiently excuses the
way the three essays overlap here and there. Nevertheless, they
fit together, it seems to me, to form one *Quaestio disputata,*
having as its starting-point, and term, the view that the particular and individual cannot be reduced to the general. This
proposition is not to be discussed here with the sense it would
bear as an abstract problem in general metaphysics. To one
reader that would seem tedious, to another platitudinous, and
to a third extremely arduous. At all events an ontological *Quaestio disputata* of that sort, if the topic were to be properly dealt
with, would demand more trouble and work than can be devoted to it here. Besides, in the end we would probably not have
convinced this or that reader, while someone else would have
the impression that we were labouring the obvious. Perhaps it
is better for once to indicate the importance of the matter for
the actual Christian life of the individual and the Church. Then,
perhaps, some would realize that it really is necessary to deal
with abstract questions more seriously than is sometimes done

[1] They were first published in *Wort und Wahrheit* 12 (1957); *Stimmen
der Zeit* 160 (1957); Fritz Wulf, *Ignatius von Loyola.* Seine geistige Gestalt
und sein Vermächtnis (Würzburg, 1956).

in scholastic manuals of metaphysics, if they saw that something does actually depend on this abstract question. Those who thought we were labouring the obvious in enunciating the abstract proposition concerning the impossibility of an exhaustive reduction of the concrete to the abstract and general, would, perhaps, realize better that these matters are not quite so obvious to everyone after all. And finally those who are not particularly interested in abstract ontology as such, but in the practical theology of Christian life and the Church, would at any rate, we think, find that they had to occupy themselves with the questions that directly concern us here.

If in the ontological domain of the person and of personal decision, the singular or particular is not purely and simply an instance of the universal, susceptible of entire resolution into it, without there remaining from this "abstraction" anything but mere limitation as such, then a difference in kind must be drawn between principles which express a universal essence, and prescriptions which are directed to the concrete particular precisely in as much as it is more than an instance of the universal. That this is so, and what it means in the life of the Church and of the age in which we live, is the argument of the first essay.

If and because what is particular and personal in this sense exists, the Church, whether as a whole or in her various members, cannot, by that very fact, be merely a Church that puts into effect general principles. There is in the Church an irreducibly unique element, historical in that sense, something over and above the fact that there is nothing new under the sun throughout the course of time, a fact all the more recognized, the better one discerns behind the "contingent" and "accidental" the unity of the essence in its purity. If in the Church there necessarily exists something historically irreducible and unique, and if this arises in the Church not by chance but from God, it follows that the Church must have a charismatic element. This is precisely the absolutely unique gift of God to the Church and to the individual in the Church, the outcome of a particular divine prescription as distinct from the carrying out (necessary and holy as this is), of the principles permanently inscribed in the Church by God, though these principles are put into concrete effect in that divine inspiration too, and are not even susceptible of realization in any other way. Consequently the charismatic element in the Church and therefore in the life of the individual member of the Church, is the theme of the second essay.

If the two first essays represent a sort of applied philosophy of concrete particulars in the life of the Church, the third is a modest attempt to provide the first two with an epistemology.[2] For the question inevitably arises from the nature of the first two parts, how these mysterious concrete particulars in the Christian

---

[2] The scope of this *Quaestio disputata* does not permit us to make express reference to works recently published that discuss or mention the subject of the logic of concrete particulars in Ignatius Loyola. At least we should like to indicate a few here: L. González, *El primer tiempo de elección según S. Ignacio* (Madrid, 1956); G. Fessard, *La dialectique des Exercices spirituels de S. Ignace de Loyola* (Paris, 1956); A. Lefevre, "Direction et discernement des esprits selon saint Ignace" in *N. R. Th.* 78 (1956), pp. 673-86; E. Hernández, "La elección en los ejercicios de San Ignacio" in *Miscelánea Comillas* 25 (1956), pp. 117-181; I. Ayerra, *Función electiva de la consolación en el segundo tiempo de elección* (San Sebastian, 1955); G. Martelet, "La dialectique des Exercices spirituels" in *N. R. Th.* 78 (1956), pp. 1043-66; M. Giuliani, "Se décider sous la motion divine" in *Christus, Cahiers Spirituels* 14 (Paris, 1957), pp. 165-86; H. Madinger, "Unterscheidung der Geister" in *Mystische Theologie, Jahrbuch* 1958, edited by F. Wessely, A. Combes, K. Hörer (Vienna, 1958).

life of the Church and of the individual Christian are to be known and recognized, if they cannot be inferred from general principles alone. Nobody surely will think it surprising that we propound the question under the guidance of a saint. In fact that will make clear to the discerning reader the point and relevance of the various topics of these reflections. It would, of course, have been possible to refer to other masters of the spiritual life instead of Ignatius, even though the history of this doctrine of individual guidance by the Holy Spirit, and of individual ethics, still more or less remains to be written. But there is no doubt that a master such as Ignatius, who cannot lightly be suspected of Illuminism, is a good patron for what is intended as an inquiry, not into history, but into actual reality.

It will, therefore, be clear enough from the start that the three items in this *Quaestio disputata* have a single theme. If they handle it each in a different manner, one very theoretically, another with an eye to the necessities of everyday Christian life, this variety of treatment will not necessarily, we hope, be unwelcome.

At certain points the theme touches on the problems raised by what is called "situation ethics". But it should be noted at once that those problems are not the subject of this *Quaestio disputata*. Every author has the right to choose his own theme. When he has chosen it, an answer to some other question should not be looked for from him. The present writer expressed his mind some years ago, before the topic was on everyone's lips, about situation ethics and the mysticism of sin, and gave a warning against them.[3] He is acquainted with the pronouncements of the

[3] *Wort und Wahrheit* 4 (1949), pp. 721-34; *Stimmen der Zeit* 145 (1950), pp. 329-342; *Gefahren im heutigen Katholizismus* (Einsiedeln, 1954); cf. also *Stimmen der Zeit* 139 (1946), pp. 260-276.

magisterium and is of the opinion that they only confirm what he said at that time. Consequently, he does not need to say more on that matter. He is concerned here with what may be termed ethics of the individual or individual morality, and takes up and carries further, reflections that have already been published. If anyone feels tempted to identify situation ethics and this present ethics of the individual, and to condemn them together, I can only request him to reflect again carefully on what is expounded here, and on the express limits that are drawn. Ultimately everything depends on the plain question, which, however, must be pursued to its roots and given a decisive answer, whether in a Christian philosophy and a theology of revelation it is permissible or not to affirm that what is particular and individual, at least when it is the personal spiritual decision of a spiritual subject, possesses a uniqueness that is not merely negative in relation to a universal and, therefore, multipliable essence, but is of a kind such as, for example, was attributed to the angels by Aquinas — without their practising a situation ethics on that account. If this question, which will frequently be the subject of elucidation in the pages that follow, is answered affirmatively, the rest follows of itself, though, of course, it throws further light in retrospect on the good grounds for the affirmative answer itself.

The inner connection of these essays was recognized by attentive readers even when they appeared separately. I might refer to the article[4] which encouraged me to bring them together and publish them as a unity. In that article, the present essays were

---

[4] "Kirche und Situationsethik" in *Herder-Korrespondenz* II (1957), pp. 531-37.

also subjected to comparison with an important interpretation of the pronouncement of the Church's official magisterium concerning situation ethics.[5] The compatibility of the essays with the official pronouncements as well as with what was admittedly in the ultimate resort only a private interpretation of these, was established.[6]

[5] F. Hürth, "De Ethica situationis" in *Periodica de re morali, canonica, liturgica* 45 (1956), pp. 137-204 (the decree of the Holy Office in *A. A. S.* 48 [1956], pp. 144 ff.); cf. also J. Fuchs, "Éthique objective et éthique de situation" in *N. R. Th.* 78 (1956), pp. 798-818.

[6] The above-mentioned article refers the reader to a book by Cardinal Lercaro (*Metodo di Orazione mentale*, Genoa, 1948; an English translation was published under the title *Methods of Mental Prayer*) which indicates the correctness and importance of this individual mode of knowledge, by the fact that it is only on its basis that even the relative necessity of the prayer of meditation becomes clear.

I

PRINCIPLES AND PRESCRIPTIONS

1. *The Distinction between the Two Concepts*

DISTINCTIONS have their uses. By them reality is more clearly seen in its variety, and relations otherwise only dimly and confusedly surmised stand out sharply. For that reason even apparently very abstract and subtle thinking about such distinctions can have its importance, provided the distinctions arrived at are really understood and, even more important, made familiar by practice for ready use. Of course, it may happen that a suggested distinction has, unknown to its proposer, long been current under another guise. He has wasted his pains; his obtuseness has served him ill. His punishment, a light one, will be that no-one will heed his suggestion. Distinctions between things that previously were seen as one and dealt with as such without discrimination cannot, of course, generally speaking, be drawn simply by inventing new words: unless it is a case of creating a new name for a tooth-paste. For them to be made and come into convenient use, people have to be induced by an analytic presentation of the matter to use two words, which until then they had used more or less equivalently, or had felt to present no contrast but to be merely disparate, discriminatingly for two things (for example, civilization — culture, fear — anguish, love — eros), which clearly stand out as objectively distinct only as a result of this analytic reflection.

We should like to put forward a distinction between principles and prescriptions. By the latter we do not, of course, simply mean imperative sentences like, "John, bring me my slippers!" We have in mind ethically important precepts, addressed to the conscience and the practical creative power of an individual, a nation or an age. It will become clear later why we cite no examples. Now it might be thought that a proposal to distinguish such prescriptive maxims from principles was an obvious matter. After all, it might be said, principles are indicative statements which express states of affairs as they are, bring before the mind the configuration of reality and as such are different from imperatives, prescriptions. But things are not as simple as this. For every matter of fact which is comprised in the nature of a thing and expressed in a "principle", also contains, when this fact can be respected or disregarded by an exercise of freedom, a claim on men, a rule of what ought to be. Consequently it might be held that every principle is always expressive, not only of what is, but also, though in varying degree, of what should be; that is, it is a prescription too. So the proposed distinction would amount to nothing.

This is where the problem really begins. It is one of fact and of terminology. It is necessary to come to perceive the factual problem and patiently to weigh the proposal to fix this in a certain terminological way, which, of course, has nothing compulsory about it. What we are saying is that not every principle, even when it is a principle enunciating what ought to be, and a valid principle and one to be followed, is necessarily by that very fact a prescription, in the terminology we are employing as more appropriate to the topic because more discriminating. Principles, one might also express it, are not in themselves solutions. What does this mean, and why is it so?

There are principles, universal propositions bearing on some nature or essence and expressing the structure of some reality, above all, for example, that of man. These can be translated into claims, demands, maxims in accord with the dynamic nature and right to existence of the reality in question. The human person of flesh and blood, for example, possesses intrinsic significance and is an end not a means, and in order to be himself and develop, stands in orderly relation to a surrounding world of material things. This state of affairs can be translated into the general maxim: The human person has a right to private property; such property should exist. Moral principles of this kind can be proclaimed, preached, defended. Men can be called upon to respect them. The unhappiness consequent on their violation can be predicted.

But are the demands that one can make on others or on oneself, and the acceptance of which would constitute "resolutions" or "decisions", solely such as follow from general principles — claims that are implied by universal propositions concerning some essence? Clearly the answer depends firstly on whether what is individual can be the topic of an obligation, of a claim to realization, and secondly on whether the individual is simply and solely an instance, a particular case realizing a universal nature, or whether it is more than this. The first of these conditions calls for no remark. It is fulfilled as a matter of course when actual spiritual persons are concerned. For all normative maxims, however abstract they may be, are not intended to defend the idea of man, but the concrete individual man; they do not make a claim on the idea but on an individual here and now in flesh and blood. Whenever a general moral principle is laid down, it is, of course, not the mere intrinsic validity of a prin-

15

ciple that is affirmed, but its realization which is demanded. Now this always takes place in a particular individual, even if in this case the individual element itself is demanded as the realization of a universal idea, an abstract essence ("man", "marriage", etc.). There is no doubt, therefore, that what is individual can be the object of a moral imperative. But the question of the second condition is difficult. For if the individual is merely the limited instance or case of the universal, so that "this" man is only "a" man, his positive reality will consist in his realizing that general nature which is the ground of moral principles. At best it will be less than the universal idea, to the degree at any rate that this not only subsumes other individuals as well as the one in question, but also leaves open at least the possibility of a greater fullness of content, so that the individual appears to be a mere spatio-temporal localization of the universal. In that perspective, an obligation relating to what is individual can only have its ground in the universal nature, and can only consist in a general moral principle or a combination of them applied to a "case" or "instance", however complicated we may suppose this to be, of some general kind.

But if the singular, the concrete particular here and now, at least when it is spiritual and personal, is more than merely one of a kind and has a positive content and individuality that is not mere *limitatio* of the universal, then precisely this individual feature can be the object and goal of a moral demand which is not identical with the validity of general principles, but is a concrete, particular, individual obligation. This is beyond the reach of general normative maxims explicative of an essence, though not in contradiction to them, for, of course, it cannot be really distinct from what in the individual is the individualized realization of the universal essence. It is the proposition which enunciates such an individual obligation that we should like to term a "prescription" and distinguish, partly as a matter of terminology, partly as a matter of fact, from moral "principles".

In fact the second condition does seem to hold. No scholastic philosopher can deny that there can be such cases, at least according to Thomism. In this view, for example, what makes the angel Gabriel is so absolutely unique, so unrepeatable, so far from being merely incidental, that God himself, though he can create many "angels", cannot possibly create a second Gabriel who would be distinct from the first merely in some numerical or serial manner, but not intrinsically. Consequently one can conceive of requirements that Gabriel has to fulfil in his being and action that are valid only for him, and which can no more be valid for others than there can be a second Gabriel. On Thomistic principles, then, with the best will in the world, one cannot deny on principle that there can be individual prescriptive norms which are in the proper sense unique. From what has been said, it is clear that this does not mean that as a matter of fact, by reason of a pattern of circumstances occurring by chance and only once, the norm for this situation finds actual application only once, though there is no intrinsic reason why the particular pattern should not recur more than once. It rather means that there is necessarily only one "case" to which this norm is applicable, and by that very fact it is no longer a "case". This, of course, in no way implies that for this absolutely individual Gabriel the principles are inapplicable which necessarily apply to a "creature", a "spiritual person", an "angel", by reason of these abstract essences. For, of course, Gabriel precisely as Gabriel is a creature, a person and so on, and these principles are integral components of his individual norm which we are calling a "prescription". But they cannot adequately express him, however subtly precise and elaborately combined we imagine them to be, if, as St. Thomas holds, "this" angel is intrinsically more than "an angel".

Now we are entitled to assert the same thing of human beings, on a variety of grounds which cannot, however, be gone into here. Though a man is subject to the law of the universal nature "man", and though as a consequence there is a general ethics deducible from this nature, an ethics of this essence, universal moral principles valid everywhere and always, nevertheless a particular man is not merely a circumscribed instance, an application of the universal. In his individual life, spiritual and free, as a being that is not wholly comprised within the material dimensions of space and time, he makes his individual eternity, finality, definitive end. And if as a spiritual, personal being he is more than the point of intersection of general truths and maxims, more than the particular instance of a multipliable essence, then this unique and special feature, this single human existence can be summoned by an imperative prescription which is different in kind[1] from the moral principles that derive from general characteristics. "Prescriptions" and "principles", even when these are expressed in the imperative form, are not the same.

---

[1] Different in kind does not, of course, mean in contradiction to, or in opposition to, or superior to general principles. This has already been made clear by the example of Gabriel Thomistically viewed. Difference in kind means that to the general nature, even thought of in the complexity of its full elaboration, something radically new accrues, namely precisely what is individual, what goes beyond being merely an instance, being one of a kind and therefore susceptible of being counted; what

It is impossible here to undertake to answer the question how this actual particular individual element is known, how far it involves a truly moral claim to realization or is merely something possible but morally indifferent; or how something of this sort can be recognized, and what formal principles can be worked out regarding this ontologically and ethically individual element. Material propositions cannot, of course, be used here, for propositions operate with general concepts even when they refer to what is individual. These and similar questions could be raised but cannot be followed up here. It is only possible to indicate that the way in which the individual element we are talking about is a datum, and known, is very different from that of the universal. A nature is usually present in a number of examples at various points of space and time and so can be subjected to experiment. It can be conceptually expressed as an object directly spoken of in propositions. But the actual individual in its particularity cannot be so grasped in conceptual and propositional form. Knowledge and love, seeing and deciding, are more inextricably interwoven in its apprehension than is the case with knowledge of the universal. Consequently its apprehension, which is very intellectual and even sublimely spiritual, can be misinterpreted as merely gratuitous assertion, as feeling and mood, as an unverifiable expression of taste, and so on.

We must also leave the question open, on what precise relation this individual element, to the extent to which it furnishes

is more than (but not in contradiction to) a universal essence circumscribed in space and time. Consequently a new obligation goes with it, even if this cannot be reduced to a general concept and so expressed, precisely because it is something that is not general.

the reason and ground of the prescription, stands to the various particular practical realizations which, in themselves at any rate, still remain possible even in the concrete, when all the relevant moral principles have been taken into consideration. To put the matter more concretely: Suppose there remains a morally open choice between several possibilities for some moral agent in regard to his duty in a particular case even though all moral criteria have been applied. For example a man X Y after analytic scrutiny of his situation in the light of all the relevant principles of general abstract ethics, after an analysis in terms of general characteristics of the case, that is, still sees it is morally permissible for him to become a doctor or a priest. How within this free scope does he discover the determining decision, "I will become this and not that"? Whichever way we look at it, it has to be arrived at. In a purely arbitrary way? (By counting buttons?) Or is there room here, always or perhaps only sometimes, for a morally obligatory, entirely particular requirement, an individual prescription? Where does it come from? From God in the sense of a direct individual vocation? From a freely made decision? From the characteristic stamp of the person as he or she actually is, considered as itself entailing a sufficient moral obligation, even if this prescription cannot be regressively reduced to general principles of morality or adequately expressed in them? The relation of the prescription to the field of morally possible decisions left open by general principles cannot be further elucidated here.

Of course, the following objection might very well be made: There may be this *individuum ineffabile* which is not merely a particular instance of something general: it may be that a certain prescriptive or normative character belongs to it if it is viewed in that way; but — so the objection runs, — if so, this is necessarily just as conceptually *ineffabile* as that of which it is the normative character, and cannot be expressed in a prescription either, because prescriptions too employ general concepts. Yet a distinction must be drawn here. It is correct that even a "prescription" cannot express and attain the individual and its uniqueness as directly as concepts and the propositions and moral principles composed with them, can express the universal, whether in itself or as it is in a particular individual. Nevertheless, a prescription has a special relation of its own to the individual as such, like a gesture pointing to "This here". Let us suppose (to take up again the example used above), that we say to someone, "You can, all things considered, still become either a priest or a doctor, because even taking into account all the circumstances of your life involved in your free decision, you are fitted and qualified for both". Such a sentence, whether intended as a statement or as a direction: "Become either a priest or a doctor, but not an actor", expresses something general about this man, his life and possible occupation. But if in the same situation this man is told by God, perhaps by a special illumination, "You must become a doctor, although you could become a priest", then this sentence, in fact, bears not merely on the general aspect of this concrete case, this life and this occupation, but also on the unique aspect of this choice of a profession and of this life. It has reference to what is concrete, and this concrete thing, said to an *individuum ineffabile,* necessarily involves the uniqueness of the concrete thing and not merely its character of being an instance of a nature, one of a kind. A definite decision, and the prescription of this decision, undeniably bears on more than the universal aspect of a concrete particular, even though, if we leave out the sheer reference pointing to the individual, it cannot actually formulate expressly more than what is universal. It also designates what is individual in the concrete particular, not just the case, the instance, but what is unique in the case, even if the case viewed precisely as a case is not unique. In other words, because the prescription implies that reference, that pointing gesture, it can stand for us here for the will and obligation directed to what is unique. It implies that gesture more than a statement sentence does, though this too can only signify a concrete particular to the extent to which it is linked with a gesture of this kind,[2] and which, of course, is not really part of the sentence itself.

Attention must, however, also be drawn to another point. The distinction between principles and prescriptions holds good not only for individual men one by one, but also for historical entities like states and other collective historical factors. These have their intrinsic individuality in time and place, their definite moment in history. Each has its καιρός, its historical task and so on. Consequently they also have their definite normative "prescriptions" and these are not to be confused with general moral principles,[3] for the two things have different ontological grounds and are not known or put into effect in the same way. In short,

[2] In order to grasp what is meant here, one need only ask oneself what sentence refers solely to Socrates as this actual concrete person. It will be found that we must think of the sentence as linked with a demonstrative gesture. Otherwise it is only possible to frame sentences which will also hold good of another and yet another Socrates, at least in another world to ours.

[3] They, of course, exist and are also valid for these unique historical things too.

collective entities on the large scale such as nations, ages and epochs, historical situations, all have their own quite definite imperative "prescriptions" which cannot be reduced to the sum-total of abstract general principles.

As regards much of what is involved here, we can only refer the reader to what we have said elsewhere.[4] We should only like to make one observation. It goes without saying that in "concrete circumstances", prudence is necessary, the virtue which enables us rightly to judge in view of these circumstances and in these circumstances, precisely what is appropriate here and now. The rôle assigned to this virtue by Aquinas is, of course, well-known, though at various times it has been almost forgotten by some moral theologians. But the question is, what is the nature of this virtue and what is its object? If one tries to answer this question, one must candidly admit that prudence first envisages the full range of general principles, then the concrete circum-stances and inquires what principle or combination of prin-ciples is to be actually applied in precisely these circumstances. That is, of course, correct and right. But the question at once rebounds. Are these circumstances only instances of abstract essences? For example, the pregnant mother whose life is threatened by her child, is threatened, it may be, to this degree while receiving such and such treatment. This is a "case". However concretely one thinks of it, it is no whit less the case or instance of a general concept; for precisely this case can be thought of as occurring as often as one cares to suppose. Or are these cir-cumstances, in addition to being instances, also something absolu-tely individual that is not attained by the application, in the way

---

[4] Cf. Karl Rahner, *Schriften zur Theologie* II (Einsiedeln, [2]1956), pp. 227-46.

we have just indicated, of a complex of general terms to something that is concrete but not really unique for all that? If so, how does prudence discern this? Besides, prudence will only be a distinct part of the human power of moral decision, one that cannot be replaced by shrewdness and erudition, moral theology and casuistry, if there is such a thing as this "inexpressibly individual" element in the concrete instance and in the concrete circumstances. Otherwise prudence would only amount to the task of popularizing the learning of moral theologians, if, that is, these latter claimed to be able, in principle though perhaps not absolutely in practice, to discern what should be done in the actual instance here and now, by their own means, that is, by general principles and their mere application to circumstances similarly resolved by analysis into general terms. The appeal to prudence, therefore, does not solve the set of problems that we have in mind, but only notifies their presence. One would have to say more precisely whether prudence is skill in disentangling the general and "essential" from the confusing yet fundamentally analysable complication of the concrete or whether it is also the capacity clearly to perceive the singular feature over and above.

Another point must be mentioned. There is no question that the Church with divine authority preaches moral principles — the reader is requested to give the word at this point the sense we have explained — principles of natural law and principles of positive supernatural law as laid down by God or by the Church. These principles of the Church regulate the action of men, or at least they should. That means, of course, the individual actions of individuals and of ecclesiastical institutions and groups. For it is precisely and necessarily in individual actions and individual achievements that general rules are transgressed or complied with. Now the proclamation of general rules, abstract ethics in the widest sense, belongs primarily to the Church's teaching office. And since these rules are addressed to the individual, and the Church seeks to get them put into practice (by admonishing, warning, passing judgment, punishing), their proclamation is also a pastoral function. It would be absurd, after all, to regard the Church's task in regard to these rules as purely doctrinal, as though it were of no further concern to her, once they were preached, what people did about them. By judging and stigmatizing, she can indubitably condemn as sinful, objectively at least, the transgression of general rules, as we see from the doctrine and practice of ecclesiastical discipline in the apostolic Church. Consequently, she has a more comprehensive function in regard to individuals than merely the abstract doctrinal proclamation of principles. In the domain of her own liturgical, sacramental and disciplinary life as such, her pastoral activity is certainly even more extensive. In this sphere, as reflection on her history in matters where she has certified that what was done was rightly done will show, her decisions are not only consequences necessarily deduced from her "eternal" principles, but true decisions, prescriptions, each of them bringing about in its time something historically unique and individual, which was not merely a particular case of the abiding abstract principles.

On the other hand it is clear that the Church is not simply of herself in possession of all the prescriptions that are practically and morally important for the individual and for states and nations. She does not impose on anyone, for example, his trade or profession and is indubitably incompetent in principle to do so, even though such a prescription is of the greatest importance for the individual and his salvation and even for herself, when there is a shortage of priests, for instance. She also expressly disclaims any direct competence in temporal matters, in the secular decisions of peoples and states, in constitutional, economic, cultural questions and so on. And if she does ascribe to herself in these things an "indirect power" (however this may be more exactly defined), in view of the moral importance of such decisions, and if by the moral law which she proclaims she puts limits to what is morally permissible in such decisions, that clearly presupposes once again that her principles and her power to forbid some concrete decisions as immoral, leave open in principle a domain within which several decisions are possible from the abstract ethical point of view. And it would not be possible for the Church herself to say which of these is the one to choose, the right one, the historically successful one. Yet the choice between these several alternatives cannot be dismissed as indifferent and unimportant, for on just this choice, which the Church declares beyond her own competence, everything may historically depend, the rise or fall of a nation or a civilization. It by no means follows from the fact that no contradiction to the general precepts of morality and therefore to their administration by the Church can be detected, that everything will certainly be avoided that might turn out historically disastrous. Otherwise, for example, the morally blameless and ecclesiastically dutiful statesman would necessarily be right in fact and historically successful in his decisions.

From what has been briefly indicated, therefore, it follows that in the life of the individual and of nations, the Church recognizes a domain of decisions, concrete individual accomplishments and consequently of prescriptions, for which as such she has no competence. This domain lies outside the scope of general principles and the Church's pastoral power. She does not and cannot relieve the individual or nations of the task of discovering such prescriptions nor of the burden of deciding. Salutary and beneficial as the general principles are which she preaches, she leaves individuals and nations, in regard to these particular prescriptions, to their own devices; they themselves must engage in the struggle to discover, choose and carry them out. Now of these, one can be the correct one, appropriate to the age and moment and the historical individuality of the agent, another can be quite the wrong one, though both may conform to general moral principles. It may not be possible to say that this only seems to be so, that in fact this apparent conformity stems not from the facts but from the agent's limited knowledge, acting as seemed good to him but objectively and in relation to general moral principles acting incorrectly.

The Church does not administer all reality. Everything indeed belongs to the kingdom of God, but not to the Church that prepares the way for the kingdom. The Church cannot say whether in France after 1871 the Bonapartists or the Monarchists or the Republicans were "right" in their prescriptions. She could enunciate neither the one nor the other of those prescriptions; she could only say that *suppositis supponendis* each of them was compatible with the general moral principles of which she is the guardian. But this would not settle whether one was historically right and the other not, nor would it settle whether all three would entail more or less the same consequences for the Church herself, the kingdom of God and the salvation of souls. All the more is this so because it is always disputable whether the necessary presuppositions that have to be taken into account in a different way each time with every historical prescriptive decision, even in order to authenticate it in the light of general principles, are, in fact, really fulfilled. Certainly it is not given to the Church to decide clearly and certainly in every case, for otherwise the Church herself could never make a mistake in practice.

The example just given may be false. For in an individual case no one, of course, can say with absolute certainty whether precisely in this instance a completely exhaustive analysis of the situation with all the relevant general principles taken into account might not after all have indicated definitely one decision as the only correct one. Obviously in many cases it is beyond the wit of man to attain this exhaustive view of all general principles and an exhaustive analysis of the situation. If this were not so there could not be any disputed cases even in casuistry where, of course, the cases are inevitably simple and tame, despite all their ostensible complexity, because they only contain what has been put into them. At all events two remarks must be made about such an example. In the first place anyone who in the concrete does not reduce a person to being an instance of a general kind, must admit that there must be cases of the sort our example was intended to typify. Secondly, it is evident from such an example, if it is carefully examined, that the very act of analysis itself alters the case — an idea of modern physics that can be transferred to this domain. The way the masses viewed the case, their interpretation, preference, taste, their individual decisions which coalesced into a collective will, were themselves also factors in the situation that was to be analysed, and this analysis itself, in the form of a proferred interpretation seeking acceptance, itself influenced the collective view of the case and so the situation itself that was in dispute. One ought really to recommend moral theologians to investigate for once in their casuistry real cases of some magnitude. For example, should the pope have attempted as early as Pius IX's time to sign the peace with Italy that later on Pius XI did? If one tried to work out cases of that sort one would very likely soon be convinced that in the actual experience of moral decisions there must clearly be a residue which is out of reach, not because of a relative, but because of an intrinsic incapacity of abstract reason. Something new must be added to that reason: inspiration from on high, the enlightenment and guidance of the Holy Spirit who does not merely ensure by an *assistentia per se negativa* that rationality functions; the historical decision which is not merely obedience or disobedience to general principles; in short the "prescription" which bears on what is unique in time and place precisely as such. Here too one would also be able to see, for example, that prayer for enlightenment does not ask God solely for help to know what we can know by the general exercise of reason.

2. Practical Consequences of the Distinction

A very concrete application may perhaps be permitted of what has been indicated so abstractly. The reader himself must judge whether to regard what follows as a casual application serving to throw light by examples on what has been said, or to envisage what has gone before as a mere introduction, designed to give precise formulation to what, at bottom, is the real intention. And here, without more ado, is the example.

In present-day Germany we have many principles and few prescriptions. Not that there can be too many principles. When they are correct — and that is taken for granted here when it is

29

a question of those the Church officially teaches — there can never be too many of them, and it is right to proclaim them. It is also evident that a lot of things would be much improved if the principles that are proclaimed were followed and that the principles are not proved false because their rejection brings misfortune. Yet those who proclaim the principles should surely also ponder why these principles when preached are so little heeded. If they answer, because it is the hour of darkness and of the power of evil, they should also ask themselves why the latter is supposed suddenly to be stronger than previously and why the "ancient truths" and "unchanging principles" are of less avail. If they explain, as is after all of greater practical importance and more correct, that the historical changes of the times with their new conditions have created new problems and difficulties which can only be overcome slowly and patiently, then they must ask themselves whether they know how these new conditions and situations are to be given shape and form so as to provide a tolerable milieu for the realization of those principles, or whether once again they would only have general principles available instead of prescriptions. Viewed in this way it is clear that the more doctrinal proclamation of general principles ought to be accompanied by a statement of prescriptions. But it must be made plain in this connection that these prescriptions themselves cannot consist of principles. "The family must be defended", "Sunday must be preserved", "The middle classes must be maintained", these and the like are correct principles, but not prescriptions. If it is said that shift-work is destructive of the family, that is very likely correct, but even such a statement is only a limiting principle that is opposed (and rightly) to a concrete (and false) prescription. For a negative is always abstract and general. If it sometimes seems otherwise, that is not due to the negation and rejection, correct in itself, of the false principle or false prescription. It is because it so happens in fact and not through the nature of the negation that there is or seems to be only one positive solution left. Consequently no positive prescription is required, or is thought to be.

Viewed from that angle, a summons to action that looks like a prescription is often simply a principle. A sentence verbally the same can even in the course of time change from a prescription into an abstract principle. "Vive le roi!" was once an imperative, a prescription, for under royal rule people could and did think of something quite concrete when they employed it. Nowadays the expression would be a royalist principle and one would have to ask how exactly and in what concrete terms the said monarchy was envisaged, for obviously a former monarchy cannot be resuscitated from the dead past any more. "Defend private property" was for the nineteenth century gentleman of independent means, and on his lips, a prescription, for he wanted to know that the actual system then existing of invested property and income derived from it was being defended. Today it is a principle. Even at that time it was an abstract principle when the Church enunciated it, although rentier and ecclesiastic both thought they were saying more or less the same thing. The corresponding prescription today would have to say what form this private property would take, how it could be defended against the propertyless forces of a managerial society, how increased and better distributed and so on.

Such concrete demands and proposals would be prescriptions. They would not be merely prescriptive, for, of course, they would also include the demand for the realization of quite definite general principles, for example, that of private property. They would be genuine prescriptions all the same, because by their demonstrative gesture designating a concrete situation and the actual effectuation of something concrete, they would necessarily also include something beyond generalities and principles, something that the general principles would be unable unmistakably to justify. It would, of course, still be possible to urge that in these circumstances this is really, in fact, the only possible way of putting into effect the binding principle in question. But those who had not already decided upon precisely this way of carrying out the generally recognized principle would dispute the claim that this realization of it was the only possible one. And in very many, if not in all, cases this claim would not be susceptible of proof nor would it fit the facts. But then we are back with principles which only come to life when they turn into prescriptions. And these do not claim at all to be principles pure and simple, not even in the sense that here and now, in themselves, the principles unmistakably require that and that alone which these prescriptions state is to be done.

If in present-day Christian Germany we examine and closely analyse our preaching and teaching, and by that we do not primarily mean the preaching of the Word of God from the pulpit, but the whole position adopted by the Church and by Christians in regard to concrete questions and decisions in the life of the individual and the nation, we must admit that there is too much talk of principles and too few prescriptions. That is why what we say often sounds well-worn and familiar, tedious, facile and almost hollow. In itself it is not. For principles must be proclaimed. But people are mostly on the look-out for prescriptions and spontaneously listen to this preaching and teaching as though it were intended to announce prescriptions, as indeed it is often wrongly supposed by the speakers themselves to be doing. People are quite right, really, to have this expectation. For the hearers are supposed to act, that is, to do something concrete, for that is the only way fundamentals and essentials and eternal truths can be carried into effect. But what they mostly hear is principles instead of prescriptions, the ideal instead of the actual model, the abstract proposition instead of a vividly depicted actual example. So what is said sounds trite, facile and empty. We propound too many principles and too few prescriptions. Consequently we give the impression of wanting to restore the past.

Our pronouncements seem too cautious, anxiously decanted, measured out. It is all very correct, but rather sterile. No one clear unmistakable note. Too much golden mean. The cart is right out in the middle of the road, well away from either ditch, but it doesn't move on. People are proud of the Catholic synthesis of principles that are difficult to harmonize and that sometimes seem almost incompatible. But it is easy to lose sight of the question how this balanced system of carefully reconciled principles, the famous "whilst on the one hand, yet on the other", actually looks in fact. For with the best will in the world, not all the actual features of our general view of things that have to be taken into account can be fully brought out to the same extent. A decision has to be made to present it in a quite definite style. For it is not the case that men with their limitations can decide from one single principle all that they have to do and carry into effect, however much they may strive to integrate the multiplicity of their nature, their tasks and principles in ever higher and richer unifying principles. Inevitably a man has a plurality of principles. To respect them simultaneously is not the result of a self-evident pre-established harmony of this plurality of principles (There must be freedom ... There must be order ...). It is only possible by a decision, and one which cannot in the strict sense be deduced necessarily as the correct one. Prescriptions are needed. Yet these are often lacking, or only the old ones are proffered, and they have already turned into abstract principles or become false, that is, historically ineffectual. Eyes are on the good old days, which, of course, could scarcely have given birth to the present if they had been as ideal as is sometimes asserted even nowadays in panegyrics of the past at the expense of the present.

We cannot undertake here to give more detailed grounds for our assertion of the lack of practical prescriptions in our present-day Catholicism. But to be honest we must admit that the mood among these Christians is dull, rather bored, listless. They don't even have any proper disputes among themselves. Unity is preserved, but preferably by avoiding ticklish questions. Things are smoothed over and settled by administrative procedures and the problems are supposed to be solved. It is not easy to make clear to the ordinary man anything really new that we want over and above, that is, the maintenance of things as they are, and apart from certain difficult moral requirements and the rejection of communism; or how we envisage the future, not the one that is just coming — "The future has already begun" — but the future that we will to come, work for and fight for. If anyone feels obliged to contradict this, he can regard the present writer as one such ordinary person, and realize from his case that there do seem to be people all the same whom the practical prescriptions have not yet reached sufficiently clearly.

If one thinks, for example, of recent Catholic congresses, one might say with a certain amount of malicious exaggeration, knowing that there are, of course, other quite different sides to these gatherings as well, that a few years ago people still wanted something definite, but now they are more cautious: they want principles to be carried out. In terms of the Spiritual Exercises of St. Ignatius one might say that they choose the abstract end, instead of racking their brains and, even more important, rending their heart over the choice of concrete means to the attainment of a provisional, of course, but quite definite goal. Let us hope the day is still distant when people say, "Such and such people in those days at least knew what they were after", or when from sheer boredom and weariness of being free and available for anything, without any binding prescription, some submit to the yoke of men who possess prescriptions even if they are false and short-sighted ones. It almost looks as if people in the Soviet Zone of Germany, perhaps only a small part but all the more valuable a part, are slowly ceasing, for these and similar reasons, to envy us in the West. Yet we are moving towards such new and difficult possibilities that it should stimulate the hard thinkers and strong hearts among Christians, each in his own domain, to possess not only abstract principles but practical prescriptions, not merely a Catholic faith but also a Christian view of things, if we understand by this not the bare sum-total of correct principles, particularly of natural law, but an organized body of correct and historically appropriate practical prescriptions.

Now, of course, a lament of this sort over the lack of prescriptions is itself a principle and even more meagre than most because a very formal one. Talk about the concrete as such is very abstract talk. Nor is it easy to remedy the cause of the lament, and for a variety of reasons. Christians in the last few centuries have come to represent the conservative principle, though that is really not something that should be taken for granted. It is not surprising, therefore, that they consider the maxims by which they in fact live as too self-evident to require much detailed discussion, or that they hold up as a reproach to their iconoclastic opponents the abiding principles, for they can demonstrate these with certainty and think, but with not quite as much certainty, that they have thereby defended the old maxims and prescriptions. Christians are on the defensive and that tempts them to defend themselves from their strongest positions. Now it is easier to cast doubt on prescriptions than on principles. Furthermore we have already seen that the Church has not in most cases the task and authority to lay down these prescriptions. Naturally she has to proclaim, for example, the fundamental moral principles of any economic system but not to recommend a particular model for a more effective economic system than the one we have. The official representatives of the Church are aware of this with greater or less degrees of clarity. The Church has already had unfortunate experiences with the recommendation or defence of particular prescriptions and maxims: the alliance of Throne and Altar, for example, and has learnt caution. She is afraid of saying things that would have to be withdrawn later. So there is a retreat into principles.

Finally, prescriptions are harder to come by than principles, especially prescriptions that are correct, practicable, opportune and effective, and most of all those that have to become those of a nation and an age if they are to be realized. It is difficult to get a prescription actually accepted as such by a social group, for it can be disputed, even among Christians, who in theory hold the same principles. Prescriptions of this kind do not, after all, present the simple alternative of being either always true or absolutely false. One can even concede them as possible in theory and yet reject them as guides in practice, even for the simple reason that one has no particular mind to do things in just that particular way. A classical education, for instance, may be a splendid thing, but no one can be obliged in the name of Christianity to have his children given one. No wonder, then, if we have difficulties over prescriptions. Moreover, none have so many principles to take into account in framing prescriptions as we Catholics have, for as "universalists" we have always the full range of true and important principles to administer, and a long historical memory that finds it hard to forget, and consequently does not find it easy resolutely to throw overboard a lot of historical ballast and go forward calmly and freely into a novel future. Commonly we have to have the ballast removed for us. Just consider, for example, the anxiety there was only a few years ago about making any changes in the liturgy, or the trouble there was before clerics in Central Europe could wear reasonable suits. For these and other reasons, then, it is easier to lament the sterility of our heads and hearts in the matter of practical prescriptions and the tedious and ineffectual invocation of general principles, than to do anything better. Only three points can, therefore, be added to this perhaps useless lament.

First of all, we should cultivate a sort of modern "probabilism", or should one say "tutiorism" — in this case it would amount to the same thing: the conviction that on the one hand we need reasonable practical prescriptions, but not such as can be rigorously proved to be the only correct and effective ones, and that on the other hand to have none at all is the worst of all.

We need the conviction that caution is something that characterizes action, not that it is a substitute for action; that one should beware of putting forward a prescription simply in order to sabotage one that has just been suggested from some other quarter by showing that it is not "inescapable". In short, an attitude needs to be built up that shuns endless "Ifs" and "Buts" and "Whilst on the one hand yet on the other" and "It is not as simple as all that". Reforms in religious orders of women, for example, although encouraged a number of years ago in the highest quarters, seem to come to nothing for the lack of an attitude of this sort. A prescription based on probability is better and surer than a merely correct abstract principle from which no action springs. Anyone who rejects a concrete proposal ought to be allowed to do so only if he produces another new prescription (not a principle) which he is willing to put into effect. "More or less everything is settled and provided for", "All that is needed is to hold fast to the excellent rules that already exist" ... that is the sort of thing the complacent brings out. Those are not prescriptions.

Secondly, we have already said that the Church in the sense of the official hierarchy has for the most part not the task of discovering and defending the sort of prescriptions we are talking about. The Church in that sense is the authoritative teaching and pastoral office of the Church, which has the doctrine of the gospel to preach and announce to every age. But that does not mean that Christians and especially the Christian laity (who are also the Church), are dispensed from the task of having prescriptions and maxims of a kind that are compatible with the gospel and the Church's teaching and at the same time form a concrete programme of Christian activity. Simply because the

Church cannot supply them ready-made and ready for use it is far from the case that Christians themselves can have a clear conscience even if they have not got such maxims, or that they cannot be morally reproached in this regard by the Church, even though direct ecclesiastical censure can, in most cases, only be directed against actions that contradict principles but not against false prescriptions or the lack of any in the life of the individual or the community. For example, it is only very indirectly or not at all that the Church can dissuade from a mistaken choice of profession or marriage, although this can be much more devastating than a sin, against which she does protest. One might express it fairly accurately by saying that the finding and disseminating of prescriptions is first and last a matter for the laity and for the apostolate that is theirs, the action of Catholics, as distinct from "Catholic Action". Here they do not and cannot simply take their orders from the hierarchy. They should not expect orders of that kind and should not think that the apostolate of the laity only begins at the point where such commands or particular wishes are expressed, in Catholic Action, for example. Here they can usually expect from the Church no direct mandate, as they say nowadays in France in discussions of these topics. It must come from their conscience and from God: whether, for example, one remains a member of such and such a union or not. The distinction between principles and prescriptions could perhaps also help to settle the question of the position and function of the layman in the Church, of the lay apostolate and of the difference between Catholic Action and the activities of Catholics as Catholics. If Christian lay people find and put into effect these appropriate and well-timed prescriptions, the Church, or Christianity, is operative in them, for, of course, they are also of the Church, yet the Church does not need to commit herself in her authoritative teaching and pastoral office. But she has to ensure, for example, through the training given in the various branches of Catholic Action, that Christians do not think they have fulfilled their duties if they are living in peace with the authoritatively proclaimed principles of the Church.

Thirdly, lay people should be encouraged and educated much more than formerly to discern the will of God even in spheres where the Church cannot tell them what it is in its actual individual detail. They should be made aware that we Christians can have a duty sometimes to unite (even perhaps at the cost of sacrifice and mental self-denial), not only on principles but also on a prescription, a practical proposition, even if this cannot authoritatively be imposed by the Church's magisterium. We should learn that it may be wiser tactics to work out a few prescriptions than always to proclaim all the correct principles all together. That supplies the humility needed for courage to be healthily "one-sided", for it is easier by the nature of the case then to blame oneself than when one is the representative of principles. We might be more serene, more confident and have more enthusiasm and sense of mission in representing practical prescriptions than we commonly are except when the big speeches are being made. The self-assurance of the followers of Moral Rearmament might to some extent be an example.

Practical prescriptions can only flourish in minds and hearts where there is proper freedom of opinion and inquiry, speech and discussion. According to Pope Pius XII, there must be a public opinion in the Church because the lack of it would be harmful to flock and shepherd. One may well think that it is not very lively, though there are gratifying exceptions. The only defence of the inheritance of the past is the conquest of the future. But for that we need, as well as much else that is far more important, practical prescriptions, not only abstract principles.

II

THE CHARISMATIC ELEMENT IN THE CHURCH

IT IS SAID that the Church was founded at Pentecost. It can also be said that Jesus established the Church by giving authority to Peter and the apostles. We hear an echo in Pius XII's encyclical *Mystici Corporis* of the view that the Church came into existence on the cross as the second Eve and mother of all the living, sprung from the pierced side of the second Adam who died there. These statements need not be in contradiction, for each graphically expresses a facet of a complex occurrence which cannot be assigned a quite determinate moment and date because it concerns a society, not a physical event. To the nature of the Church there belongs her structure as a society hierarchically organized with a variety of offices and authorities, and also the Spirit animating her like a soul, as well as the manifestation of this gift of the Spirit, for she has to bear witness through history precisely as such a Spirit-endowed society. Consequently, mention is made of the cross, as the event in which in the Blood of the Redemption the Holy Spirit is given to mankind, and of Pentecost, when it is made known tangibly and by testimony that this Spirit has truly come.

1. The Charisma of Office

The Spirit is promised and given to the ecclesiastical ministry. The promise that the Lord will remain in his Spirit with the Church all days until the end of the world also applies to the official Church. For if that were not guaranteed by the power of the promise, the official hierarchy of the Church as such could revolt against God and against the truth and grace of Christ, could fall away from God, lose his grace. In that case she would really only be like the Synagogue which, founded by God in the covenant, broke the covenant. The Church would not be the new and everlasting covenant, the Church of the last days against which the gates of death cannot prevail. At all events she would not be the visibly hierarchically-constituted Church of the apostles, with her mission and discipleship, her ministry and Scripture, her written word, her visible sacraments, the Church of the Word made flesh. It would still be possible, of course, to hold even then that there was a "Church", in so far as there were, and always would be, men seized and possessed by the Spirit that blows where it wills, so that the Church would ever be springing up anew. But that would not be the one abiding historical entity founded on the apostles and their enduring mission, remaining always the locus and visible manifestation of grace, its sacrament. Consequently the Spirit must be assured to ecclesiastical office as such, and so it is that the apostles and their disciples following them in historical succession are told that the Lord will be with them all days until the end of the world. It is not that men and the office they hold and their law are not in themselves in a position to rebel against the Spirit of Christ and to disown that Spirit, nor as if the Church, consisting as she does of men and therefore of sinners, were incapable of becoming the synagogue of Antichrist. But because the grace of God is not only offered to mankind as a possibility, but is promised to the Church as a victorious grace more powerful than sin, it is certain from the outset from God's side and from him alone, that ecclesiastical office in what most properly belongs to it, in its essence, will not, though it could, be used by men as a weapon against God. To that extent, therefore, ecclesiastical office and ministry is charismatic in character, if we understand by charismatic, what is in contradistinction to what is purely institutional, administered by men, subject to calculation, expressible in laws and rules.

That ecclesiastical ministry does not rebel against God and his Spirit, that in the last resort it does not abuse its power and force against God, cannot be ultimately ensured by anything pertaining to this power itself as a juridical, tangible element. There is no question of lodging an appeal against an alleged abuse of this power with some other tangible court of appeal, nor of stirring up a revolution against this ministry by claiming that it has unmistakably and confessedly offended against the spirit and the letter of its foundation, so that in consequence it has lost its *raison d'être*. And yet, because there is no section in the official constitution of the Church to which one could appeal against official authority and so be freed from its jurisdiction; and because the ministry cannot exclude by merely human means the mortal danger of an abuse of ecclesiastical authority that would destroy that authority itself; and because the official Church must, for all that, be preserved by God's grace against fundamental abuse, there belongs to ecclesiastical ministry as such a charismatic element, transcending the institutional order. It is usually referred to among us Catholics as the assistance of the Holy Spirit that is accorded to ecclesiastical office and those who hold it. It is important, however, to be clear in one's mind what is involved in this simple statement. It implies that this assistance cannot entirely be reduced to juridical terms. It is not to be identified with the divine wisdom of the Church's laws, though both as principles of jurisprudence and as precepts of morality they prevent many abuses. It cannot be adequately translated into those laws. For, of course, there is no judicature in the Church where an appeal might be lodged from men to men, and there is no right to revolution. The first would abolish a human and tangible supreme court of appeal in the Church altogether, while the second would be a denial of the Church as an enduring visible historical entity with genuine continuity.

This is clearly to be seen, for example, in the fact that the highest seat of jurisdiction in the Church, the pope, also possesses competence to determine what his competence is. If he invokes his highest and ultimate authority, it is not possible to oppose his decision with the claim that he has exceeded his powers, acted *ultra vires,* and that his judgment is not binding on that account. For it is not possible to verify that he has kept within the scope of his competence by applying a criterion to him, as though by judicial process, to test his conduct. When he invokes his ultimate authority in making a decision, this action is itself the only guarantee that he has remained within the limits of his competence. But that means that such an office held by a human being, if it is not to be an absolute tyranny, must itself rise into a sphere to which no judicial criteria can be applied. It must necessarily itself be charismatic. And that means it is only conceivable if there is always added to it in fact and in idea a power which is itself indefectible, the assistance of the Spirit of God himself, permanently promised to it, even though this is not something that can be administered or comprised in legal terms.

Here, therefore, is an office which in order to be what it is, passes into the charismatic sphere. Consequently we also have

45

here a case where the charismatic feature has not simply the character of being merely sporadic, intermittent. "Charismatic", "irreducible to juridical terms", "given only now and again", are not the same thing. For that very reason, however, the "charismatic" retains its incalculable character. That is taken very much as a matter of course by a Catholic. He can only conceive the right functioning of an office, even of the highest in the Church, as the office (if we may so express it for the sake of clarity), acting in accordance with its true structure. He can very easily think of the office as functioning rightly because God so arranges things that it does not act, that the individual holder of office dies, that some power or other, external to it, impels it unexpectedly to act in a way different from what it would otherwise have done. It is clear, then, that according to Catholic belief the guarantee of the unfailing rightness of official action lies not in an intrinsic feature of the office as a human, juridical, tangible entity, but in God's assistance alone, and this can make use of every conceivable means, not necessarily connected with the office itself. Of course, all this does not mean (and for our further reflections later it is important to stress the fact), that the office in each of its manifestations is markedly "charismatic".

The theology of the Church has worked out with ever-increasing clarity when, to what degree and with what varying certainty this charismatic assistance of the Holy Spirit is promised to the Church's ministry. That is not our subject here. Every Catholic Christian knows, for example, that the charisma of infallibility only belongs to papal teaching authority under very definite, clearly determined conditions. Everyone knows that the Church in the exercise of her pastoral office, in her legislation, administration, adaptation to the requirements of the sage, pastoral practice, in her activity in art, learning and the shaping of Christian life in practice, can exhibit faults, omissions, partially mistaken developments, signs of sclerosis, reactionary tendencies. But it would be incompatible with the invincibly Christian character and holiness of the Church and contrary to an ecclesiastical spirit to maintain that, though infallible in her teaching, she is not, in her normal life and activity, under the guidance and direction of the Spirit promised to her; or if one wanted to hold with a sort of mental obstinacy (there are such people), that more or less everything is wrong that the Church has in actual practice done in the course of history, except her solemn dogmatic definitions, — as though the life of the Church amounted to practically nothing but sin and falling away from the mind of Christ. Such people may imagine they have a heroic love for the Church, of the "in spite of everything" sort. In fact, they consider themselves to possess a mind of superior discernment to that of the actual average everyday Church. They do not believe in the charismatic character that belongs to the Church's ministry even in the world of every day, even under the routine of what is laborious and unpretentious and commonplace.

All this is merely intended to make it clear that office and spiritual gifts in the Church cannot be conceived as two totally distinct elements which happen to be united more or less by chance in a person who is endowed with office and yet at the same time with a charisma. Office itself and not merely the actual man who in fact holds office must be characterized by charismatic gifts if the Church with its hierarchical constitution is to remain to the end the Church of the abiding Spirit, which through God's grace alone is incapable of falling in its totality from the grace, truth and holiness of God and of so turning the visible representative manifestation of grace (for that is what the Church is) into a synagogue devoid of the Spirit.

2. The Non-institutional Charismata
a. The thesis

It would be just as false, however, if one were to suppose that the charismatic element in the Church is reserved to her official ministry. There are, in fact, earnest Catholics who are anxious to have a right mind about the Church and who hold the view, tacitly and in the background, but all the more operative and dangerous on that account, that the hierarchy is the only vehicle of the Spirit or the only portal through which the Spirit enters the Church. They imagine the Church as a sort of centralized state, and a totalitarian one at that. We must distinguish between what we may perhaps for our present purpose call an absolute claim made by the Church ,valid within certain limits and strictly circumscribed, and a totalitarian conception of the Church. For the Catholic the Church is absolute in the sense that he knows that the Church is the enduring and imperishable home of his salvation, the ground of truth, the inexhaustible well-spring of grace, the representative of the visible presence of Christ's grace until the end. And all this refers to the hierarchical Church. Consequently, for anyone who has once accepted by faith this Church as the measure of his life, there is no point of vantage outside this Church from which he might oppose her, no court of appeal to which he might take a claim against her. If he struggles and argues with her, it is a struggle and a debate within the Church herself. He is speaking to the human members and ministers of this Church and appealing to guiding principles and a spirit which they recognize as their own and to which they concede they are themselves subject and willingly subject. For a Catholic every "clash" with the Church is always an occurrence recognized by the Church herself as an expression of her own life and only to the extent that it is such a thing.

In that sense, therefore, the Church is an "absolute" for the Catholic. Simply because she is one with Christ, who for him is the Absolute made man, and because she declares herself to be one with Christ. Here again, it is part of this faith in the union of the Church with Christ that she does not transgress the limits set to this unity (although there is a perpetual temptation to do so), in the spheres where as bride and handmaid she is distinct from her Lord and stands essentially apart from him. But this attribution of an absolute character does not involve a totalitarian view of the Church. Such a conception would be totalitarian if anyone were to think, explicitly or tacitly, that the Church is not liable to err in any of her actions, if it were supposed that all living impulses of the Church can and may only originate from her official ministers, that any initiative in the Church is only legitimate if it springs expressly or at least equivalently from above and only after it has been authorized, that all guidance of the Holy Spirit always and in every case affects ecclesiastical office, God directing his Church only through her hierarchy and that every stirring of life in the Church is the mere carrying out of an order or a wish "from above". Such a false totalitarian view inevitably equates office and charisma, if any importance is left to this latter. But this is just what is not the case. For there are charismata, that is, the impulsion and guidance of God's Spirit for the Church, in addition to and outside her official ministry.

Now this thesis is not a private opinion but a doctrine taught by the Church's own magisterium, a doctrine of Scripture itself, and a truth lived and practised in the Church in every age, though this does not prevent its being more clearly and more explicitly realized by the Church's human members at certain times.

b. The Church's teaching

Pius XII wrote in the encyclical *Mystici corporis:* "But it must not be supposed that this co-ordinated, or organic, structure of the Body of the Church is confined exclusively to the grades of the hierarchy, or — as a contrary opinion holds — that it consists only of 'charismatics', or persons endowed with miraculous powers; though these, be it said, will never be lacking in the Church . . . . But when the Fathers of the Church mention the ministries of this Body, its grades, professions, states, orders and offices, they rightly have in mind not only persons in sacred orders, but also all those who have embraced the evangelic counsels and lead either an active life among men, or a hidden life in the cloister, or else contrive to combine the two, according to the institution to which they belong; also those who, though living in the world, actively devote themselves to spiritual or corporal works of mercy; and also those who are joined in chaste wedlock. Indeed, it is to be observed, especially in present circumstances, that fathers and mothers and godparents, and particularly those among the laity who co-operate with the ecclesiastical hierarchy in spreading the kingdom of the divine Redeemer, hold an honoured place in the Christian society, and that they too are able, with the inspiration and help of God, to attain the highest degree of sanctity, which, as Jesus Christ has promised, will never be wanting in the Church . . . ." Christ "established that authority, determined by appropriate precepts, rights and duties, as the primary law of the whole Church. But our divine Saviour himself also governs directly the society which He founded; for He reigns in the minds and hearts of men, bending and constraining even rebellious wills to His decree. . . . And by this interior government He, 'the shepherd and bishop of our souls', not only cares for each individual but also watches over the whole Church: enlightening and fortifying her rulers so that they may faithfully and fruitfully discharge their functions; and (especially in circumstances of greater difficulty) raising up in the bosom of Mother Church men and women of outstanding sanctity to give example to other Christians and so promote the increase of His mystical Body." (*A.A.S.* XXXV [1943], 200ff.; *C.T.S.* translation, *The Mystical Body of Jesus Christ* [London, 1948], pp. 13-14; 23-24).

If we reflect attentively on this teaching, it is possible for us to say that there are persons in the Church endowed with the charismatic gifts of the Spirit outside the sacred ministry. They are not merely recipients of orders from the hierarchy; they may be the persons through whom Christ "directly" guides his Church. Obviously office is not thereby abolished. The Lord, of course, guides and rules his Church, the same encyclical tells us, through the medium of the sacred ministry. Holders of office themselves can receive, in addition to the authority of their charge and its proper administration under the protection of the Spirit, direct impulsions of that kind from the Church's Lord. But if Christ directly operates in his Church apart from the hierarchy, if he rules and guides the Church through charismata that are not linked to office and in this sense are extraordinary, and if, nevertheless, there is a valid and irrevocable official ministry in the Church, then harmony between the two "structures" of the Church, the institutional and the charismatic, can only be guaranteed by the one Lord of both, and by him alone, that is to say, charismatically.

Now it is no doubt a rule, a normative principle and a law for the spiritual gifts themselves, that they should operate in an "orderly" way, that they are not permitted to depart from the order prescribed by authority. As a consequence it is possible to use as a criterion of their authentic spiritual origin the fact whether or not they do this. Yet this formal rule alone would not of itself guarantee the actual existence of harmony. For though official authority might be sufficiently protected by the rule from merely apparent spiritual gifts, the charismata also need to be protected from the authorities. Provision has to be made that bureaucratic routine, turning means into ends in themselves, rule for the sake of rule and not for the sake of service, the dead wood of tradition, proud and anxious barricades thrown up against new tasks and requirements, and other such dangers, do not extinguish the Spirit.

No really effective remedy against them is ensured by the formal principle that official authority must not extinguish the Spirit, any more than it is merely by the punishment that in the long run always falls on authority if it trusts more to the letter than to the Spirit. The effective guarantee is not given by official authority and its principles alone. Even though the authorities can only sin against the spiritual gifts by transgressing the very principles of their own authority, it is not thereby excluded that those in office might not discern their own principles clearly enough in the matter, that they might do prejudice to them and be in danger of excluding the charismatic element from the Church as a nuisance. Safeguard that is effective and certain to be effective is only to be looked for from the Lord of both. He is the transcendent source of both, and he himself is the support that he promised to his Church always and victoriously, consequently he can ensure the unity of the two elements. Their unity cannot itself be institutionally organized, it is itself charismatic, though this charisma is promised to the Church as one that will endure till the end. It will have to be considered presently what practical conclusions follow from this fundamental idea, which is based on the papal teaching about spiritual gifts and immediate relationship to Christ on one hand, and the institutional component of the Church on the other.

We must add another remark here concerning the texts quoted above. Spiritual gifts need not necessarily and in every case occur in a miraculously extraordinary form. Every genuinely Christian life serves the Body of Christ, even if it is lived in an "inconspicuous" (rather than "unimportant") place in the Church. It is the charismatic features of the Church as a whole which must in addition be of a striking character. For the Church, of course, is to be by her inexhaustible plenitude of holiness a sign set on high among the nations, and herself the proof of her divine origin and mission, as the First Vatican Council taught (Denzinger, *Enchiridion Symbolorum,* No. 1794). St. Paul too assumes the same (for example in Galatians 3:2), for by the charismata the pagan is to recognize and acknowledge in adoration that "God is among you indeed". But that does not mean that because the Church's charismatic character functions as a mark of credibility, the spiritual gifts in her individual members must necessarily be something extraordinary. Leaving everything else out of account, there is heroic fidelity in commonplace, everyday things, the miracle of balance that hides its own miraculous quality in the serenity of the obvious. The Church teaches that even the lasting observance of the natural law, that is, of what belongs to the accomplishment of human nature as such in this world, requires a special help from God which in fact, ultimately speaking, men only receive from the grace of Christ. Consequently even the preservation of purely human moral excellence points, objectively speaking, to the power of grace. How much more, therefore, is this true of what exceeds the average manner of life such as is "generally" led, even if this feature that goes beyond the average appears very simple and not particularly noticeable precisely because of, not in spite of, its extraordinary and therefore, in our case, charismatic character.

We cannot here expound the teaching of St. Paul concerning spiritual gifts in the Church: see in particular 1 Corinthians 12–14; Romans 12:1–8; 16:1; Ephesians 4:1–16. The mere reference must suffice.[1] By way of summary of it, one might perhaps say that, for Paul, ecclesiastical offices can be spiritual gifts, but there are others. He regards ministries and other functions in the Body of Christ which by their nature cannot be institutionally administered, in the same perspective as gifts and tasks which the Spirit distributes, supports and combines, despite their diversity, for the life and well-being of the one Body of Christ. But at all

[1] E. A. Allo, *Première Épître aux Corinthiens* (Paris, 1935), pp. 317–388; B. Maréchaux, *Les charismes du St. Esprit* (Paris, 1921); D. Th. C. IV, 1728–1781; D. B. Suppl. I, 1233–47; H. J. Brosch, *Charismen und Ämter in der Urkirche* (Bonn, 1951); O. Karrer, *Um die Einheit der Christen* (Frankfurt, 1953), pp. 50–90.

events, and this is what is decisive for our purpose, Paul does not recognize only spiritual gifts that are bound up with office, ministries that are gifts of the Spirit both as office and as pneumatic enablement to fulfil the office. He recognizes other spiritual gifts as well, and recognizes them as just as important for building up the Body of Christ. Furthermore, these special charismata need not necessarily always concern extraordinary mystical things. The simplest help, the most commonplace service can be a charisma of the Spirit. Another striking fact is that Paul does not oblige the theologian by distinguishing between a *gratia gratum faciens* and a *gratia gratis data,* that is, between a grace that makes its recipient himself intrinsically holy and pleasing to God, and a grace only given "gratuitously" to someone for the benefit of others and the Church generally but which does not sanctify the recipient. Not that such a distinction is not possible and in many cases appropriate. Jesus himself, of course, drew attention to men who work miracles and yet displease him. But Paul does not make the distinction. On the contrary he only sees or only envisages the case where the charismata both sanctify the recipient and redound to the benefit of the whole Body of Christ simultaneously and reciprocally. It is a very evangelical way of looking at it. For how else could one truly sanctify oneself except by unselfish service to others in the one Body of Christ by the power of the Spirit? And how could one fail to be sanctified if one faithfully takes up and fulfils one's real and true function in the Body of Christ? If both are done, and that by God's Spirit, inconspicuously perhaps but in a truly spiritual way, that for Paul is a charisma of the Spirit of the Church, and it belongs just as essentially to the body and life of the Church as the official ministries.

Since this is noted by Paul and by the pope, is it really so very obvious that theologians in their treatises on the Church may simply say nothing whatever about it? Yet that is what they do. In the outstanding new treatise on ecclesiology in the Spanish textbooks of dogmatic theology by Joachim Salaverri, for example, which goes far beyond what is usual with us in Germany in content, precision and bibliographical information, there is not a word about the charismatic element in the Church. All we find is a refutation, and rightly, of the theory of Sohm that any juridical element in the Church is in contradiction to her original charismatic conception. Of course, the charismatic element in the Church is not denied by theologians' thinking they do not need to waste a word on it in their treatises on the Church. To them it seems too self-evident. But when supposedly obvious things are passed over in silence[2] or it is considered they are no doubt dealt with elsewhere and from other angles with other concepts, there is considerable danger of their being overlooked. That will become clearer when we raise the question what practical conclusions emerge from what has been said.

Since these practical applications have unavoidably a certain critical character, we may perhaps point out beforehand the following, which is also stressed in the encyclical *Mystici Corporis,* and which represents the third proof that the charismatic element belongs to the essence of the Church: This charismatic element has always, in fact, existed in the Church.

[2] In H. Haag, *Bibellexikon* (Einsiedeln, 1951), we read, col. 541: "Yet the gifts of the Spirit do not belong to the essence of the Church. This is not primarily charismatic but institutional, that is to say, built up on the apostles and their authority." One can see that the pope is after all more

56

Unfortunately people have become accustomed to some extent to attributing to the early Church a certain charismatic endowment which is supposed to stand in contrast to the history of the later Church and not any longer to be found so often, and no longer to be so necessary (as Gregory the Great rather regretfully added even in his time). Now there is no doubt that the early days of an historical structure, its first beginnings which are the foundation of all that comes later, have a unique task to fulfil, when something truly historic and with enduring identity is in question. The moment of first love is unique and irrecoverable, just as summer or autumn cannot be like spring. Even the mind's maturation in time cannot preserve eternal youth just as it is when one is really young. But the "charismata of early days" and "more charismata" are not the same thing. It is not clear what grounds there are for saying that the early Church was, in fact, more charismatic. Everything then was concentrated into a smaller space and consequently more noticeable. But even in the early Church not everything was charismatic enthusiasm. Moreover, the New Testament is an account which inevitably and quite rightly gives more attention to the great and holy events than to the human weaknesses that there certainly were even then. It goes without saying that as the Church grew, its "machinery" grew too, and the regulations for this were worked out more fully. But this is no proof that in the early Church the wind of the Spirit blew with more vigour than later.

"progressive" than a progressive biblical dictionary of this sort. Can that objectively false statement really be justified by saying that it presupposes a more restricted conception of the charismata than ours?

In fact, there has always been the charismatic element in the Church. We must glance into Church history, though more into the hidden everyday history than the official, "great" Church history. If in doing so we reflect on fundamental principles rather than enumerate facts, that is legitimate within the framework of such considerations as these. Church history is not here being studied for its own sake.

The Spirit has always held sway anew in the Church, in ever new ways, always unexpectedly and creatively, and bestowed his gift of new life. He has never abolished official authority and laws, which after all derive from one and the same Spirit, but again and again brings them to fulfilment in ways other than those expected by the "bureaucracy", the merely human side to office, which exists even in the Church. And he has again and again brought the hierarchy and the whole institutional element to recognize this influence of the Spirit. That is not the least of his repeated miracles. The love of martyrdom was a charisma which existed side by side in the early Church with cowardice, calculation and compromise. Charismata too were the numerous waves of monastic enthusiasm which led to ever new religious communities from Anthony and Pachomius down to the many smaller foundations of the nineteenth century, even if many such later foundations appear to have sprung more from shrewd, almost secular, aims and from a need for organization, than from an original impulse of the Spirit.

3. The Possibility of Institutional Regulation of a Gift of the Spirit

With regard to such charismatic enthusiasm for the evangelical counsels, which can only be followed through God's grace, it must be realized that not only the first emergence of such a mentality, which, of course, nearly always forestalls or occurs apart from and indeed, to all appearance, in spite of the institutional elements in the Church, but also the institutionally organized transmission and canalization of such gifts and graces of the Spirit, belong to the charismatic component of the Church. Not only Francis but the Franciscans too are charismatics if they really live in a spirit of joyous poverty. What would Francis mean to the Church if he had not found disciples throughout the centuries? He would not at all be the man of charismatic gifts in the sense we have in mind here, but a religious individualist, an unfortunate crank, and the world, the Church and history would have dropped him and proceeded with their business. But how could he possess disciples, many disciples, who have really written into the actual history of the Church something of the ever-young grace of the Spirit, if these disciples and the soul of the poor man of Assisi had refused on principle to be faithful to this Spirit of theirs under the yoke of ecclesiastical law, of statutes, vows and the obligation that derives from the liberty of love? It is precisely here that it is clear that the charismatic element belongs to the Church and to her very ministry as such. She has the courage, the astonishing and impressive courage, and many holders of office may well not realize what they are doing thereby, to regulate the charismatic element in the Church's life, to formulate "laws" concerning it, and to "organize" this Spirit. You have someone trying to do what according to the gospels is only possible by God's gift, what one can only "take" if it is given from above, something that proclaims that the form of this world passes and that the last hour has already struck. He is offering his heart to God, that it may only think the things of God; telling God that in the

59

adventure of love for him and as an expression of faith, he will renounce earthly love in marriage. He acknowledges this love for God. And the Church listens, receives this profession, administers it, binds the man who has made it, holds him to it in God's name. She is convinced, therefore, that the man who has made it has been taken at his word by God, that he truly possesses the charisma of Christian virginity. She knows, therefore, that God, because the Church does not release him from this obligation, (which is after all that of his love), will also give him the grace to keep his promise. The Church lays down rules for such a life, makes a state of life out of this spiritual gift, similar to, or rather proportionately similar to the difference of status between the sacred ministry and those who hold no office. In the Latin Church she even combines her ministry and the state of life of celibate charismatics (at what a tremendous risk), and consecrates as her priests only those who declare in conscience before God that they have the grace to be able to take this venture upon themselves. She holds these consecrated servants of her sanctuary to their word and never releases them (though she could) from this obligation.

The Church must be very conscious indeed in this, her institutional and official activity, that she is the charismatic Church. In this she shows the sternness of exuberant life and the inexorability that is a sacred necessity of the greatest things. She knows that only too often, as far as we can see, ultimate fulfilment and maturity is denied to such charismatic enthusiasm, that the holy venture of voluntary poverty, of a holy renunciation of earthly fulfilment, of contemplation in silence and obscurity, is only blessed with meagre fruits. And so it may sometimes seem as though the Church, harsh to the individual and his perhaps tragic lot, were only using such abundance of idealism for her own ends. It is not possible to conceive the official Church and hierarchy as the institutional organizer and administrator of the gifts of the Spirit in the Church, unless one sees her from the start as being herself, she the law-giving Church, first and foremost the Church of the charismata.

The sixteenth century Reformers did not intend, of course, to reject the evangelical counsels as such, at least that was not the first intention; Scripture attests them too plainly. And it was only liberal rationalism of the eighteenth century sort, with little understanding even of the faith of the Reformers, that thought itself obliged to be cleverer and wiser than Scripture in these matters. But what the Reformers could not see, was that things of that kind could have anything to do with the visible Church and her officials and laws. They envisaged the Church in such a way that the hierarchy was really only a human form of organization, even if an unavoidable one, to meet religious needs. The Church of the later Middle Ages whose official ministries conducted themselves in a far from charismatic manner, did not make it easy for them to see her otherwise. And so for them spiritual "office" properly speaking was only to be found where the gospel is preached in such a way that it pierces the heart in judgment and justification. A ministry of which even the theory was secularized in this way could obviously not claim to "administer" the evangelical counsels which are a spiritual gift. On those premises, such a rejection is understandable. If the ministry were no more than an institution belonging to this world (even though established by God, like the authority of the state, for example), it could not, in fact, "administer" the free charismatic gifts of the Spirit. Anyone who can only see ecclesiastical office in that way, as an external expedient of an external order, and not as the efficacious sacrament of inward grace, cannot admit that the Church regulates and administers the evangelical counsels, but must deny that to follow them in the Church can constitute a "state of life".

4. Lesser and Greater Spiritual Gifts

To return, however, to the point we had reached in our reflections. The Church throughout her history has always been charismatic. The excursus we have just made was perhaps not superfluous, if it has clarified what that means. For from that it follows that if the official Church is also the guardian and guide of the charismatic element, if she herself possesses the gift of discernment of spirits, then the charismatic element is not to be looked for solely in what is very rare and extraordinary; that is practically beyond the reach of such guidance and only needs it in a very indirect and general way. It is not, of course, as if everything to do with God and his Spirit can and must be regulated and realized in the same way. There is certainly a domain which cannot be directly administered by the Church,[3] but we cannot simply identify this with the realm of the spiritual gifts and so degrade the official Church into an external, bureaucratic, administrative machine. Our excursus can serve to indicate that in the Church there is much more that is charismatic than one might at first think. How many human beings in the Church keep alight in the cloister the flame of prayer, adoration and silence? Is the intensity and magnitude of this phenomenon, even when one

---

[3] See K. Rahner, *Gefahren im heutigen Katholizismus* (Einsiedeln, ³1955), pp. 11-38: Der Einzelne in der Kirche.

includes all its human and mediocre and ossified elements, all the dead wood, something to be taken for granted? Or is it astonishing, a grace and a miracle?

From this point our view broadens out into the history of the charismatic element in the Church and it becomes clearer that this seldom if ever means something that in the normal outlook of a secular historian would require to be given special prominence. It is not necessarily the case either, we hasten to add, that this grace-given charismatic element must necessarily be found only within the bounds of the visible Church. The idea of special spiritual gifts, at least when each individual case is viewed separately, does not include that of being an exclusive privilege. Consequently if in what follows we point out charismatic features in the Church and the impression is formed that such things after all exist outside the Church as well, and even outside Christianity, that is no argument against what has been said. For the Christian knows, confesses and feels it in no way a threat to the uniqueness and necessity of his Church, that there can be and is God's grace and the grace of Christ outside the Church. He does not prescribe to what heights that grace can raise a human being without, and before, incorporating him or her into the sacrament of grace, the Church. It is not even by any means settled in theology that any instance we observe anywhere in the world of the observance of the natural moral law, even in a single act, is, in fact, only a natural act without the supernatural elevating grace of Christ, even though it is not performed by a Christian from consciously supernatural motives. It is quite possible to hold that as a matter of fact in all or nearly all cases where a genuine spiritually and morally good action is actually accomplished, it is also, in fact, more than merely such an act.

The grace of Christ surrounds man more than we think, and is deeper, more hidden and pervasive in its application in the depth of his being than we often imagine. It is quite conceivable that wherever a human being really affirms moral values as absolutely binding, whether expressly or merely in the actual unreflecting accomplishment of his nature, intrinsically orientated as this is beyond and above itself towards the absolute mystery of God, he possesses that attitude of authentic faith (even if only virtually),[4] which together with love, suffices for justification and so makes possible supernatural acts that positively conduce to eternal life.

If this is taken into account, it becomes even clearer that we have no right to assign arbitrary limits to the grace of God outside the Church and so make spiritual gifts and favours simply and solely an exclusive privilege of the Church alone. But on the other hand this does not mean, either, that we are not permitted to see the charismatic element in the Church where it really exists within her, not in the great pages that belong to general world history merely, but in hidden fidelity, unselfish kindness, sincerity of disposition and purity of heart, virile courage that does a duty without fuss; in the uncompromising profession of truth, even when it is invidious; in the inexpressible love of a soul for God; in the unshakable trust of a sinner that God's heart is greater than ours and that he is rich in mercy. All that and very much more of the same kind is by the grace of God what it really is, and what only the believer can correctly appreciate in its full profundity and endless significance, for the unbeliever under-

---

[4] See on this point K. Rahner, *Schriften zur Theologie* III (Einsiedeln, 1956), p. 429.

estimates it. It is the work of grace and not of the human heart, which of itself alone would be evil, cowardly and empty.

Now are there not things of that kind everywhere in the Church, over and over again? Have we any right to observe morosely that they really ought to be even greater, more splendid and more powerful? At bottom, of course, we often don't want to see and experience such greater things out of genuine love of these holy possibilities of mankind, but because we ourselves would have a more comfortable and agreeable time in life if there were even more of such divine goodness in the world. Isn't it often rather our own egoism we should blame for our being so blind to the splendid things there are, that we act as though it were all a matter of course, or of no importance? If we had real humility and goodness we would see far more marvels of goodness in the Church. But because we are selfish ourselves, we are only ready to see good, good brought about by God, where it suits our advantage, our need for esteem, or our view of the Church. But this unrecognized goodness, and even charismatic goodness, is found in the Church in rich abundance. That is not altered by the fact that more is brought into God's barns than is consigned in the pages of newspapers, and magazines, histories of civilization and other such human halls of fame. Can it not be charismatic goodness to be a patient nursing sister, serving, praying, and asking nothing else of life? That does not mean it is always so. Nor need one fail to recognize that even genuine virtue is rooted in temperament, social origins, custom and other pre-moral conditions, just as a beautiful flower grows from mould. But only a blind and malicious mind can no longer see, on account of the imperfection of all human things, or because of the facile discovery that even the most authentic moral excellence has its antecedent non-moral conditions, that despite all that and in it all, there can be charismatic goodness and love, fidelity and courage.

Persons of that kind, who cannot thankfully admire this goodness effected by the Spirit in the Church, and outside it, might inquire whether they themselves accomplish the things they refuse to think remarkable. Consider a mother's life. It is no doubt true that she has a narrow outlook, instinctive care for offspring drives her on; probably she would not have a much better time in this life if she were not so devoted a mother. That and more of the same kind may be true and in many cases is true. But just as life on the biological level presupposes chemistry, yet is more than chemistry (even though many theorists fail to see this), so it is, proportionately speaking, in these matters. There are good mothers whose virtue is from God above, a gift of the Spirit and of his unselfish love. And there are many such gifts of the Spirit that are the charismata in the Church. The ones mentioned are only meant as isolated examples. It is in these that the life that most truly characterizes the Church is accomplished, not in culture, the solution of social questions, ecclesiastical politics, the learned treatises of theologians, but in faith, hope and love, in the longing for eternity, the patience of the Cross, heartfelt joy. Ultimately the whole Church is only there so that such things may exist, so that witness may be borne to their eternal significance, so that there may always be people who really and seriously believe that these gifts here on earth and hereafter in eternity are more important than anything else. It remains true, of course, that men are frequently required to do these apparently small things of eternity among apparently greater temporal matters. And it is true that what has been said must not be made a pretext and easy excuse for narrow-minded mediocrities who lack this and that quality but flatter themselves that they are citizens of heaven because they are simply second-class citizens and philistines on this earth, and who want to award the "common man" a halo that he doesn't deserve in a matter where a more aristocratic awareness of difference of level and achievement would be more authentically human.

Of course, if it were a question of writing a history of the charismatic element in the Church, one would have to speak more explicitly than has so far been done here about the great spiritual gifts, about the great saints in whose creative example quite new possibilities of Christian life can be seen; about the great figures of Church history who walked like true guides and shepherds before the people of God on its journey through this world of time and led it into new historical epochs, often without realizing themselves what they were doing, like Gregory the Great who himself was expecting the end of the world and yet became the father of the Middle Ages in the West. Of the great thinkers and writers, too, who took up again the ancient Christian view of life and succeeded in so expressing it that a new age could make that Christianity its own. And the great artists who did not speak about the religion in which God became a man of this earth, but gave it visible shape, representing it in ever new forms and so actually and concretely represented something which, without such corporeal embodiment, only too easily asphyxiates in the mere depths of conscience or evaporates as it were into unreality in the abstractions of the mind. In other words, one would have to speak of all in the Church who had a special, unique historical mission of great import for the Church and through her for the world. It goes without saying that no detailed account can be given here of all these great charismata.

Now, to add another fundamental observation, these charismata are not only properties of the Church's essence which only the eye of faith perceives (all the charismata are that), but they are also criteria that convince and lead to faith, by which the Church is to be recognized as a work of God. This is not the place to go into the difficult question, one of the most important questions of Fundamental Theology, how and on what presuppositions such criteria of true belief can be recognized by human reason, which, in faith, has to perform a "reasonable service", *rationabile obsequium*. What is the rôle and scope of reason and of deliberate reflection expressible in rational terms; what is the function of grace; how do the light of faith and rational grounds of faith mutually support one another in the actual accomplishment of faith? This general problem has a particular application here from the fact that the charismatic element in the Church is not only an object of faith but by its plenitude and enduring presence and its perpetually renewed vitality, can be a motive of faith. Here we can only stress this fact. The first Vatican Council, taking up a thesis of Cardinal Deschamps, emphasizes (Denzinger, 1794) that "The Church herself is a great and enduring motive of credibility and an irrefutable testimony to her divine mission by her wonderful growth, eminent holiness and inexhaustible fruitfulness in all good, and by her Catholic unity and unshakable stability." By the nature of the case this implies that the great charismata of the Church in her temporal and spatial unity and totality, in which these gifts appear to the gaze of the unprejudiced as a special characteristic of hers, are not only an object of faith but also a motive of faith.

Of course, the use of this motive of faith in apologetics is not perfectly easy. The matter cannot, however, be pursued here. We discern the limits of something that was emphasized earlier, that there are gifts of the Spirit even outside the one visible Church. What we have said does not, however, mean that the situation of the Church is simply the same as that of the Christian and non-Christian world outside the Church. The eye of faith and the human mind seeking faith with the support of grace can recognize that the charismata which are found everywhere have, nevertheless, in the Church their home and native air and their most intense historical development, because more than any other historical entity she proves herself to be, again and again and ever anew, the Church of the great charismata.

5. The Consequences

a. Toleration of a charisma by official authority

If the structure of the Church is of this double kind and if her harmonious unity is ultimately guaranteed only by the one Lord, then office-holders and institutional bodies must constantly remind themselves that it is not they alone who rule in the Church. We have already sufficiently emphasized that God's Spirit will ensure that they do not rule in that way and in decisive matters will not wish to do so. But this fact in no way means that temptations to the contrary never arise or that such a maxim is superfluous because its final accomplishment is guaranteed. Neither the efficacious grace given in God's salvific acts nor the indefectible promise to the Church of the assistance of the Holy Spirit renders such a maxim superfluous. It is important for office-holders and their subjects, too, to keep it clearly before their minds. Both must realize that in the Church which has this charismatic element, subordinates are quite definitely not simply people who have to carry out orders from above. They have other commands as well to carry out, those of the Lord himself who also guides his Church directly and does not always in the first place convey his commands and promptings to ordinary Christians through the ecclesiastical authorities, but has entirely reserved for himself the right to do this directly in a great variety of ways that have little to do with keeping to the standard procedure and the "usual channels".

In the Church there are not only movements that have to owe their origin to higher authority in order to be legitimate. The official hierarchy must not be surprised or annoyed if there is stirring in the life of the spirit before this has been scheduled in the Church's ministries. And subordinates must not think they have nothing definite to do until an order is handed down from above. There are actions that God wills even before the starting signal has been given by the hierarchy, and in directions that have not yet been positively approved and laid down officially. Canon law concerning equity and the force of custom *contra* or *praeter legem* might be thought out from the point of view of this charismatic element in the Church. By such concepts canonists not only leave legitimate room for humanly significant development in the law, but also for the impulse of the Spirit, even if and in spite of the fact that these points in the Church's body can also, of course, become the focus of infection by the all-too-human element. Executive authority in the Church must, therefore, always cultivate the awareness that it is not, and may not be, the self-sufficient planner, as though in a totalitarian system, of all that is done in the Church. It must keep alive the consciousness that it is a duty and not a gracious condescension when it accepts suggestions from "below"; that it must not from the start pull all the strings; and that the higher and, in fact, charismatic wisdom can sometimes be with the subordinate, and that the charismatic wisdom of office may consist in not shutting itself off from such higher wisdom. Ecclesiastical authority must always realize that a subject's duty of obedience, and the fact that such authority has competence to determine what its competence is, neither makes the subordinate devoid of rights as against authority, nor guarantees that every action of authority in the individual case is correct and the one willed by God.

b. The "democratic" Church

Seeing that there is a divinely-willed dualism of charisma and office of a permanent kind in the Church, then, the "monarchical" Church, with its authority deriving from above downwards, has, nevertheless, also something of the nature of a democracy — the opposite of a totalitarian system. The name does not matter and nowadays to some people the word democracy will not seem a special title of honour, seeing that everybody everywhere is supposedly in favour of democracy even if we in the West use it to mean precisely the opposite of what is called by that name elsewhere. But if we do consider what ultimately constitutes a democracy, it is, of course, not a voting paper in everybody's hand (for those voting papers when collected together can be very tyrannical), but a society where no single authority holds all power combined, where there is a plurality of really distinct powers, so that the individual always knows he is protected to some extent by one from the excessive power of the other. In this sense every healthy state has been a pluralist state and consequently to that extent democratic. Under any constitution such a concentration of power can occur that, in fact, freedom is abolished, though that is not to say that it is equally easy, whatever the written constitution, for freedom to be abolished by a monopoly of power.

This helps us to a better grasp of what characterizes the Church's constitution. It is "undemocratic" because her office and authority, being founded directly by God himself, have for mankind final jurisdiction in their own domain. There is no absolute right to resistance or need for it in that domain, because God himself guarantees that the authority will not abuse its formal right in a materially decisive way. But there is not on that account in the Church any absolute monopoly of real power at any one point, that is, in this case, in her hierarchy. Not because that sort of thing is, in fact, never altogether feasible (it is not so even in the cruellest and most ruthless tyranny), but because it is contrary to the very nature and purpose of the Church as embodied in her ministry itself. This does not aim even on principle and in intention at gathering to itself all real influence. It sets limits to itself and this limitation which allows due scope to other forces of a non-official kind is itself guaranteed by God. To that extent, therefore, the Church is a hierarchical system, but only because its summit is God, and likewise a system in which power and authority are distributed, that is, a sort of democracy though of its own special kind.

From what has been said it is clear that even in the Church, something can originate from among the people. Not from the people of this earth merely, but from the people of God in the Church, the people of God that is guided directly by God. Consequently there is also quite rightly something in the Church of the nature of a popular element. A religious study of this popular element that regarded itself as a genuinely theological study could begin at this point to define its nature and importance. To the extent that the host of believers, where it is united in heart and soul, can be the point of entry for guidance from above, it is possible in certain circumstances to discern the Spirit of the Church in it and in what it does and feels. It, of course, remains true and goes without saying that this people is the people of God, existing in the society of the Church organized by Christ, and consequently can never stand in fundamental contradiction to the ecclesiastical authority which gives it social form and structure. There have repeatedly been times in the Church's history, the eighteenth century Enlightenment, for example, when many a gift of God's Spirit to his Church was better preserved by this simple and prayerful people than by many of the "princes of the Church".

c. Inevitable disagreement in the Church

If by her very nature there is necessarily a multiplicity of impulsions in the Church, then a legitimate opposition of forces is not only, in fact, unavoidable, but is to be expected and must be accepted by all as something that should exist. It is not just to be regarded as a necessary evil. Only impulses that in the human sphere flow from a single source cannot be felt to be "dialectical", opposed. But when in the Church's case various influences flow from God into the Church, some through the ministry, others directly to members of the Church who hold no office, it is clear that God alone can fully perceive the meaning, direction and divinely-willed purpose of these. If for no other reason than that man, being finite even as a member of the Church, makes his plans in relation to what he cannot foresee. A number of forces like this within the Church here on earth must be felt by human beings themselves as disparate and opposed, precisely because they are unified by God alone. Of course, it is true, as Paul says, that the various gifts of the one Spirit must work together harmoniously in the unity of the one Body of Christ. But since the gifts are one in the one Spirit but do not form one gift, that unity of the Body of Christ itself is only fully one in the one Spirit. For the rest it is true that no one singly forms the whole. No one has every function. Whatever the breadth and the will to wholeness, to understanding, to assimilation, the plurality of special gifts cannot be abolished.

Ultimately only one thing can give unity in the Church on the human level: the love which allows another to be different, even when it does not understand him. This makes it more understandable that charity is not only present in the Church as though in a container, but itself belongs to the actual constitutive elements of the Church, in contradistinction to all other societies. For only then can the Church be one in spite of her dual structure. The principle that charity brings with it implies that each in the Church may follow his spirit as long as it is not established that he is yielding to what is contrary to the Spirit; that, therefore, orthodoxy, freedom and goodwill are to be taken for granted and not the opposite. Those are not only self-evident human maxims of a sensible common life built on respect and tolerance for others, but also principles which are very deeply rooted in the very nature of the Church and must be so. For they follow from the fact that the Church is not a totalitarian system. Patience, tolerance, leaving another to do as he pleases as long as the error of his action is not established — and not the other way round, prohibition of all individual initiative until its legitimacy has been formally proved, with the onus of proof laid on the subordinate — are, therefore, specifically ecclesiastical virtues springing from the very nature of the Church. We have an example of this attitude in the *Codex Iuris Canonici,* canon 1323, § 3: It must be proved not presumed that a theological proposition has been solemnly defined.

We must learn, then, even as members of the Church, to let others be, even when we do not understand them, even when one has the "feeling" that they don't think as one "really" should, that is, according to one's own particular dispositions. It follows that there must be schools and trends in theology, in the spiritual life, in church art and in pastoral practice. Anyone who does not admit this is tacitly asserting that there could be a place in the Church from which all those matters were directed in detail, authoritatively, in a way binding on all and in all, so that all other persons would be merely the executors (and of a most passive and repetitive sort) of quite definite detailed views and commands. But that is just what is not the case. Even in theology it is not so; even, that is, in theory, which after all is more susceptible of unanimity than practical matters are. Of course, there are always naïve and over-enthusiastic souls whose secret wish and ideal is, in fact, represented by what the opponents of papal infallibility at the time of the first Vatican Council always painted on the wall of their untheological imaginations as a nightmare danger, namely that the infallible pope might simply settle all theological questions by his infallible pronouncement. One should ask oneself for once just why, strictly speaking, that really will not do, seeing that after all he has authority for something of the sort. If one attentively considers the simple and rather foolish question, one realizes that it is really the case, as we noted above, that the plenary powers of the highest authority in the Church, which are not subject to the check of any other human court of appeal, are not by any means the whole source from which, and in accordance with which, that highest authority acts. There belongs to it too the assistance of the Holy Spirit, which cannot be completely expressed in juridical terms, and his guidance in the actual exercise of those plenary powers. Moreover, in the present case it has to be noted too that human truth in fact is of such a kind that even in theology to settle one question, even correctly, raises three new questions that remain to be settled. Only simple-minded people fail to realize that, and think the pope, if he were only willing, could change dogmatic theology into a collection of defined propositions. For that matter it is only necessary to glance into Church history to see that there has never been a trend in the Church which in the long run was wholly and solely right and triumphed to the exclusion of all others. And trends or programmes only put themselves completely in the wrong when they put themselves outside the Church in schism. One alone has always been completely right, the one Lord of the Church who, one in himself, has willed the many opposing tendencies in the Church.

What has been said would be quite misunderstood if anyone drew the conclusion that everything in the Church must be left to go its way, that no one may have the courage to offer opposition to another trend in the Church, to utter warnings against it, to challenge it to real and serious combat. Such a view would, of course, amount to denying that the different kinds of movements and tendencies truly do develop within the one Church so that each must be balanced by the others. It would also involve maintaining that no tendencies can appear in the Church except as a gift of the Holy Spirit. But this is false. So we must also be able to have the courage (for this can be the precise function given by the Spirit to a particular member of the Church), to say No in the Church, to make a stand against certain trends and spirits, even before the official hierarchy itself has been alarmed. In fact, such a protest can be God's means of rousing his ministers to act. One must have this courage, even if one must tell oneself, knowing the limits of one's own judgment, that probably the further history of the Church will show that one was not entirely right, that one was only one servant among many of the one Lord of the Church, and not the only one to represent him, in fact, that the Lord was also acting in that other person whom one had the task of putting in his place, and convincing of his limitations.

d. The burden of a charisma

That is why a charisma always involves suffering. For it is painful to fulfil the task set by the charisma, the gift received, and at the same time within the one body to endure the opposition of another's activity which may in certain circumstances be equally justified. One's own gift is always limited and humbled by another's gift. Sometimes it must wait until it can develop until its *kairos,* its hour has come, when that of another has passed or is fading. This painful fact is to be viewed soberly as an inevitable consequence of there being one Church and many gifts. If the words are taken seriously and not emptied of meaning, "many gifts" implies that one person has a gift that another has not. How could that other person show an understanding of a gift that is only possible to its possessor who is called to exercise that precise function in the Church? Even supposing we had all the goodwill and tolerance that we could or should have, it would still not be possible to show another and his gift and task that understanding and enthusiasm which he expects and is tempted to claim his mission justifies and requires. Outside the Church the man with a mission may, of course, be misunderstood and persecuted, but he can flee to those who esteem him and recognize his mission and a community can be founded and centred on this mission. In the Church this is only possible to a much more limited extent, for example by the founding of an order or similar social structures in the Church which are legitimate and derive part of their meaning and justification from this need for social response to a new mission. In general someone in the Church who bears the burden of a charismatic mission to the Church and for the Church, must remain in the circle of his brethren. They will tolerate him when things go well but perhaps reject him and in any case show little understanding of him. The authenticity of a charisma, which after all is for the Church and into the Church, not out of her, is shown by the fact that the person so endowed bears humbly and patiently this inevitable sorrow of his charismatic endowment, builds no little chapel for himself inside the Church in order to make things more tolerable, does not become embittered but knows that it is the one Lord who creates a force and resistance to it, the wine of enthusiasm and the water of sobriety in his Church, and has given to none of his servants singly the task of representing him.

Two observations must be made on this theme of the burden of a spiritual gift in the Church. One is, that to suffer opposition to the charisma within the Church is no proof against the mission from above and the authenticity of the gift. Certainly the Church has the right and duty of discernment of spirits even to the point of completely rejecting a claim that this or that spirit is from God. But that does not mean that every contradiction, delay, distrust that is aroused in the Church or her authorities against a charisma is itself a sign that this prophet has not been sent by Yahweh. The criteria for distinguishing between the legitimate opposition of the Church to a deceitful spirit and false enthusiasm on one hand, and the painful resistance of the Church to the mission of her own Spirit in a true "prophet" on the other, are known in their main features and need not be expounded in more detail here. They are the rules which the Church and her theology lay down regarding her teaching authority, its various levels and their binding force, and the equally discriminating rules about ecclesiastical obedience. In this respect another thing must be said. To apply these rules correctly in more difficult cases is itself a charisma, a special gift. For who can tell always and at once, precisely and definitely, when self-defence of a charismatic mission against the mistrust, difference or hesitation of holders of ecclesiastical office, or even against their actual opposition, is a sign of higher charismatic insight and fidelity to his own mission, and when an attitude of illegitimate revolt against ecclesiastical authority? Why, for example, were the Jesuits right in acting as they did when they resisted Pius V's attempt to impose solemn choir-office on them? Why were they not breaking their own rules of thinking with the Church? Why was it a praiseworthy action on the part of the representatives of devotion to the Sacred Heart not to allow themselves to be put off by the rejection which they first met with from the Holy See? How often can one really remonstrate with the competent authority with petitions, pressure and so on, without by that very fact offending against the ecclesiastical spirit? When is as minimizing an interpretation as possible of an ecclesiastical prohibition, in order to continue to preserve as much room and freedom of movement for an endeavour that has the appearance of contradicting it, quite definitely compatible (as even the practice of the saints shows), with an ecclesiastical spirit, and when not? Such questions show (and that was their only purpose here), that it can itself be a special gift given only to the humble and brave, obedient yet independent and responsible saint, to discern where the burden of opposition to a mission is the cross which blesses a genuine mission and where it is a proof that the endeavour has not its origin in God. There too it is clear that it is not possible completely to comprise in plain rules of law the stirrings of the Church's life, that a charismatic element remains.

The second thing to be said about the burden of a charisma is that the inner necessity that links charisma and suffering in the Church, of course gives no patent to the authorities, and others devoid of special gifts, to be lacking in understanding, and blind and obstinate. Sometimes one has the impression that there are people in the Church who infer from Gamaliel's words (Acts 5:38ff.), that the authenticity of the Spirit is shown by its not being extinguished by the most frivolous and malicious opposition from other people, and that consequently they have the right to put the spirit to the test on the largest possible scale. Of course, it is not possible to extinguish the Spirit in the Church, God sees to that. But it is quite possible for a human being by his sloth and indifference and hardness of heart to extinguish a true spirit in another. Not only is it possible for grace to be without fruit in the person for whom it is intended, through his own resistance, but it can be given to someone for another's benefit — it is then called *gratia gratis data* or *charisma* — and remain without fruit because rejected by the person for whom it was given, although it was faithfully received by the one who received it on another's behalf. We must not be Jansenists in our doctrine of the charismata, either, and hold that all these special gifts must be given as *gratiae efficaces,* infallibly producing their effect. There are also gifts which through men's fault remain without effect for the Church. Gamaliel for that matter drew from his maxim the contrary conclusion to that of the people we have in mind. He inferred that one must be as tolerant as possible towards a spirit whose origin one cannot yet clearly make out. Ecclesiastical authorities cannot, therefore, do wrong on the grounds that a spirit will triumph in the end even against their opposition, if it really comes from God. Otherwise they cause suffering beyond what is unavoidable, do wrong to God, to those endowed with spiritual gifts and to the Church.

Anyone even slightly familiar with the history of the Church knows of sufficient examples of suffering of that kind by those gifted by the Spirit. St. John of the Cross was thrown into a horrible dungeon by his own brethren, St. Joan of Arc died at the stake, Newman lived for years under a cloud, Sailer of Ratisbon was denigrated in Rome by another saint, Clement Maria Hofbauer, and only became a bishop when it was really too late, Mary Ward was for a long time in the custody of the Inquisition and yet, of course, she was right about her mission, nevertheless. In the controversy about the nature of the love of

God, Fénelon was disavowed, not without reason, by Rome, but his adversary Bossuet who seemed to have triumphed was not much nearer the truth than his less powerful opponent. In her foundations St. Teresa of Jesus, certainly to her great sorrow, had to undergo much persecution on the part of ecclesiastics, and use a lot of ingenuity and ruse in order to succeed. From the beginning of the Church down to the present day there have been great and small instances, of these and similar kinds, of the sufferings of the charismatic individual, and there will continue to be. They are unavoidable. They belong to the inescapable "necessity" of suffering by which Christ continues to suffer in his members until the end. And he willed that these his members should also cause one another to suffer.

e. The courage to receive new gifts

A final remark by way of conclusion. One must learn to perceive such charismata when they first appear. Jesus himself observed that the children of those who killed the prophets put up monuments to them, but this did not reconcile him to the prophets' fate. It is good and has its uses if the prophets are renowned and canonized when they are dead and their charisma has been officially recognized. But it is almost of greater importance to perceive such gifts of the Spirit on their first appearance, so that they may be furthered and not choked by the incomprehension and intellectual laziness, if not the ill-will and hatred, of those around them, ecclesiastics included. That is not very easy. For the institution is always the same and develops, to the extent that it does develop, from the palpable, unambiguous principles it embodies from the outset — though this is not to dispute the creative and spontaneous element even in the juridical development of the Church, at least in its *ius humanum*. But the charismatic is essentially new and always surprising. To be sure it also stands in inner though hidden continuity with what came earlier in the Church and fits in with her spirit and with her institutional framework. Yet it is new and incalculable, and it is not immediately evident at first sight that everything is as it was in the enduring totality of the Church. For often it is only through what is new that it is realized that the range of the Church was greater from the outset than had previously been supposed. And so the charismatic feature, when it is new, and one might almost say it is only charismatic if it is so, has something shocking about it. It can be mistaken for facile enthusiasm, a hankering after change, attempted subversion, lack of feeling for tradition and the well-tried experience of the past. And precisely those who are firmly rooted in the old, who have preserved a living Christianity as a sacred inheritance from the past, are tempted to extinguish the new spirit, which does not always fix on what is most tried and tested, and yet may be a holy spirit for all that, and to oppose it in the name of the Church's Holy Spirit, although it is a spiritual gift of that Spirit.

III

THE LOGIC OF CONCRETE INDIVIDUAL
KNOWLEDGE IN IGNATIUS LOYOLA

1. *Introduction*

IT DOES NOT seem unfair to the achievements of the great commentators on the Spiritual Exercises of St. Ignatius Loyola to
say that an account of the actual theology of the Exercises is
something we still lack, at least on the scale we cannot but wish
to have today. It may be that the great commentators on the
Exercises in past centuries satisfied their own times, but it
remains true that every age must re-think standard works such
as the Exercises afresh from its own point of view. To take quite
a small example, who would deny that it is with quite different
eyes and new astonishment that we find in Ignatius' well-known
prayer *Suscipe Domine,* freedom put before the three powers of
the soul. For now, in the age of the existential philosophies,
"freedom" signifies more than one of the ways in which one of
the various powers of the soul can react. And if we realize more
clearly today and advert more explicitly to the fact that theology
is the statement of a *history* of salvation in which God in ever
new and incalculable ways has dealings with man, then the
perspective of the history of redemption in which Ignatius
places for us the meditations on the three sins or on Christ's
kingdom, suddenly becomes more than merely a skilful teacher's
device for bringing vividly home to us truths which hold good

always and everywhere and which could also be expressed more abstractly; something more than general, self-evident guiding principles of ethics drawn from the essence of man.

But we are still far from possessing such a theology of the Exercises, despite the considerable beginning made by Erich Przywara in his three volumes of *Deus semper maior*. At the start of such undertakings there is always a question, and the courage to ask questions of that kind. First, habit has to be broken, and the feeling disturbed that in such historic books, after all, it is only a matter of pious platitudes which though very useful for leading a good life, no longer hold any excitement for a theologian. He, of course, knows long since what such works of edification say, even if he is willing to concede mildly and benevolently that it is very nicely put, in a "psychologically" effective way, edifying and practical. But that is just what is not in question here. Of course, there is an edifying literature found more or less everywhere in the hands of all and sundry which, in relation to high theology, is derivative and merely repeats in simplified form what is already to be found in the theology text-books of the schools.

But there is also a literature of spirituality which stands in a different relationship to learned theology and it is not only Holy Scripture and the pronouncements of the Church's magisterium that belong to it. It is a literature of piety which forestalls theological reflection, which is more fundamentally spontaneous than the latter, wiser and more experienced than the wisdom of the learned, a literature in which the Church's belief, the Word of God and the action of the Holy Spirit, which never ceases to be operative in the Church, find more authentic expression than in the treatises of theologians. This is a spiritual literature which is not only the minting of theology for the common run of the faithful, not merely a minting of the Church's belief and the Word of God in the sense that it could be predicted by anyone interested and clever enough, but which is, rather, a "creative", original assimilation of God's revelation *in Christo*. It occurs as a creative prototype in accord with historical circumstances, and by way of example, as a new gift by God's Spirit of the ancient Christianity to a new age. In order to do justice to the importance of such books, one must, of course, have some feeling for the difference there is between repeating a process of thought, recapitulating it after another, and its first discovery by creative originality; and some awareness that however intelligible and obvious an idea may be afterwards, its first unmistakable appearance is, nevertheless, always a marvel of God's Spirit operative in history. He has his times and seasons and his "prophets" who are made of different stuff from the disciples of the prophets and teachers in their professorial chairs. One must have an inkling that it is the almost unavoidable fate of such authentic thought to be weakened and diluted in subsequent exposition *in usum Delphini,* until what at first was a great light becomes a candle giving a cosy glow to Everyman's little room.

The Spiritual Exercises belong to that kind of spiritual literature. What originally occurred with them was not really an event in the history of ideas that could be inserted, if we were so to choose, in the "Tridentine" or "Baroque" period, or in "modern times" (now coming to an end).[1] It was something

---

[1] We should like to express the opinion (without being able to give detailed grounds for it here) that Ignatius has something almost of the

of exemplary value in a quite fundamental way, for an age that is only just starting. If this is correct, the Exercises can form a subject of tomorrow's theology, in a certain sense be one of its sources, not, of course, like Scripture and the magisterium, but in the sense that everything that is a concrete realization of Christianity, yet is not fully deducible from abstract theological principles alone,[2] has something to say to theology which this cannot otherwise come to know. Once seen, it is at once recognized to be a possible realization of the nature of Christianity which theology must think over. What makes it extremely

archaic and archetypal about him. That explains what at a first superficial glance one might call the mediaeval features of his spiritual character. He has nothing that really belongs to the Baroque or the Renaissance about him. The features that are held to justify interpretation in those terms, his individualism, deliberate reflection, his almost technically regulated self-mastery, his silence and discretion, his subordination of the highly self-aware person to the objective task, the slight scepticism which pervades everything though without lyrical self-expression or self-conscious melancholy, these and similar traits are not really "Baroque" and "modern", even if in other connections the distinguishing mark of the "Baroque" and of "modern times" is the individual's awareness of himself as individual, exulting in himself or intoxicated with his own problems and complexity, a self-mirroring individuality. None of that is to be observed in Ignatius. And so in regard to what is most his own, his day seems to us still to come. But to prove that, one would have to sketch a prognosis of what the characteristic features of the age that lies before us will be. We cannot undertake that here.

[2] That there are such individual ways of realizing Christian life in the individual human being (and consequently even more in each of the various historical periods taken as wholes) which cannot be completely reduced by regressive analysis into abstract principles, is itself a proposition not immediately evident to everyone from the start, and which was, as a matter of fact, "taught" by Ignatius.

difficult for the theologian to make the Exercises an object of theological study in that way, that is, to put questions to them as a theologian in order to expound them by actually learning from them, not merely to expound them in terms of what he knows independently of them, is that the Exercises speak a language which is a downright provocation to theological pride to find nothing behind them but what has long since been known, and at most to assert that clumsily-worded and obscure passages need to be illuminated by the light of his own theological wisdom.

Let us be honest! When we theologians hear mention of the old tradition that the Exercises were composed under a quite special inspiration of the Holy Spirit, either we don't at heart really believe it, or we so restrict the assertion that it in no way affects us, and we can say that the real marvel of the book is that a man who had not at that time studied theology did not break the rules of theology. And we concede that for that matter he made practical and skilful use, very skilful use even, of what, nevertheless, he had really learnt from us, even though he got it through the little runnels of the catechism and what works of piety there were. But if we hold there are books in Christendom which, though they draw all their life from tradition and in a sense only seek to repeat it to us, are, nevertheless, underivative, the marvel of a concrete and yet really new embodiment of the unchanging essence of Christianity; and if we consider the Exercises to be one of them, then the attitude of theology to the book will be different. The theology of such a Christianity can be written. At least it would present a task, and one that could only begin if one destroyed the appearance of platitude, of tedious familiarity, if one asked questions of the sort that are not sent into the world already supplied with their complete answer.

So if a few, far from all, questions are here propounded that the Exercises raise for a theologian who takes them seriously, the reader should not take it to be idle ingenuity, nor should he complain if a ready-made answer is not supplied at the same time. Only one thing is asked of him, to take the Exercises seriously and not to start with the tacit assumption that in them there cannot be anything more than what theological speculation has dealt with long ago.[3]

2. *The Problem of the Election in the Spiritual Exercises*

There is general agreement that the nature of the Exercises is ultimately determined by the fact that a choice, a vital decision, is to be made in them. They are not a book of edification, a compendium of asceticism and mysticism, not a doctrinal work at all which states directly and for its own sake what is the case. The Exercises are guidance, regulations, instructions for something that is to be done by them. And what is to be done is to discover God's will in a decision to follow that will. All that

[3] With this limited purpose (everyone is permitted to choose his own theme) and in view of the space available, it goes without saying that it cannot be our purpose here to engage in an elaborate study of the sources for the life and writings of St. Ignatius and to expound and discuss the teaching of the commentators on the Exercises. Such things are necessary too. They are, in fact, more important than what we are doing here, and they alone can really accomplish the task to which a quite unpretentious stimulus is intended here, where a question and only a question is propounded, even where, in order not to become too monotonous, it assumes the form of a firm statement.

they say is only meant as instructions for this transaction, even when theoretical truths of the catechism are apparently expounded. This contention, which could be supported from the biography of St. Ignatius and from the text of the Exercises, probably calls for no further proof here.

But this is just where the real question arises. In what way is this discovery of God's will for each individual human being meant and envisaged? For Ignatius, of course, it goes without saying that the field in which this will of God can be discovered is delimited by the faith of the Holy Roman Catholic Church, comprised within her binding doctrine and the moral principles she prescribes for her children and puts into practice. But this involves yet another question too. How, in fact, is this antecedent delimitation of the possible field of God's will compatible with the direct utterance of this will by God himself, when God works directly with his creature?[4] If this latter exists, why is the external regulative principle not *ipso facto* superseded in principle or reduced to the level of a merely secondary means or instrument that happens, in fact, to be made use of by God?

But this problem must not occupy us yet. The question turns rather on the discovery of God's will. What happens in this

---

[4] What does it mean, for theology, if one takes it seriously that during the Exercises the Creator and Lord himself (in contradistinction to mediation by human co-operation), "imparts" himself to the faithful soul, and that "the Creator works directly with his creature and the creature with its Creator and Lord"? (*Ex. spir.* n. 15). What does it mean when prayer is made for God to "put" his will in the soul (n. 1880)? This immediate direct relation to God is, after all, in view of the Church, the institutional element of Catholic Christianity, not simply something self-evident, providing one does not dilute or whittle away this immediacy till nothing remains of it.

discovering of the will of God? In what does it consist? What is discovered? To put the matter even more precisely: In the Exercises, is an Election, made with the assistance of the Holy Spirit and by means of the technique recommended by Ignatius, only necessary because in certain cases it is difficult as a matter of fact to discover what is right, though in reality this right course is merely the logical inference to be drawn from the general principles of natural and supernatural morality, which are already known all along, and from the person's actual situation which is likewise a definite datum even if hard to evaluate? Or is it necessary to discover the will of God because it is not possible fully to know what is willed, here and now, by God, simply by way of a Christian use of reason (principles of reason and faith plus analysis of the situation), because a man must take into account on principle and not merely as a hypothetical case not normally met with in practice, that God may make known to him some definite will of his over and above what is shown by the Christian use of reason within the framework of Christian principles applied to the particular situation? The word "fully" should be noted. It goes without saying that with an Election (we will return to the point), all the principles of general abstract ethics, of universal natural law, of the moral precepts of the gospel must not only be observed, that is, may not be infringed, but also must exercise a positive, discriminating, directive function. The only question is whether that is all that is involved and whether it is sufficient.[5]

---

[5] Consequently the author of these unpretentious observations has not the remotest intention of turning Ignatius into a modern existentialist for whom the human existent, without essence of a general and communi-

That there are at least particular cases in which the second alternative is realized cannot be doubted by a Catholic, for he believes in the possibility of a manifestation of the divine will (not derivable from the universe and its principles and facts) which may concern the individual as such and his individual decision. Without that conviction, belief in a free revelation by his Word, in the sacred history of redemption, of the living personal God, is impossible. Nor has the assumption been seriously doubted in the Church in the course of her history, either in theory or practice. Not in practice, for it is clear, for example, that Christians, the authorities of the Church, the teachers of asceticism and mysticism, have always reckoned with such cases as for instance St. Catherine of Siena, St. Margaret Mary and others, to whom God in the proper sense revealed definite tasks as his will binding on them and of which they could have known nothing apart from such a revelation.

In regard to the Exercises the question rather is whether Ignatius reckons on the second hypothesis being more or less the normal case for the Christian, at least for those he is concerned with in the Exercises?[6] Or does he regard a will of God of this

cable kind, directs himself in glacial solitude, inexpressibly, with the help of an absolutely individual ethics of the human predicament and the concrete situation, if indeed with any ethics at all. But we are of the opinion that Ignatius cannot be subjected to the alternative either of being a pure existentialist or of only knowing and living, in regard to the reality of Christian life, of free decision before God and the discovery of the divine will, what can be comprised within the contents of an ethics of universal essences, necessary and important as this is.

[6] Ignatius, of course, is far from considering even all those who wish to undertake the Exercises as being really suited and capable. On this see *Ex. spir.* n. 6;9;18;19;189; *Constit. S.J.* IV 8 E; VII 4 F. Further sources are

kind, and its discovery, as an exception to which he perhaps
alludes in passing as a marginal phenomenon of asceticism and
mysticism but which is not really important for him in the
Exercises? If this is to be answered in the first way, a double
question arises for the theologian. How does he explain and
justify such a view in the light of ontology, philosophy of
existence and theology, in other words has he already sufficiently
thought about the matter generally? And then on that supposition how exactly are St. Ignatius' Rules for making the Election
to be interpreted and justified? Now we do think that the main
question we put requires an affirmative answer.

As far as I know, the similarities and differences between the
alumbrados of the early sixteenth century in Spain and Ignatius
have not yet been studied in detail, at least in German. If nowadays the former receive more justice than they did from many
theologians in their own time (as is stressed for example by
B. Colunga),[7] it will not be misleading not to exclude on principle from the start a certain similarity of outlook between them
and Ignatius, that is to say, in the conviction that there is a real
guidance by the Holy Spirit.[8] There is no need to fear an un-

---

indicated in A. Feder — E. Raitz, "Ignatius von Loyola, Geistliche
Übungen", Ausgabe B (Freiburg, 1940), Appendix, p.17 note 5.

[7] See *Lexikon für Theologie und Kirche* I (1st. Edit.), pp. 326 ff.; I (2nd.
Edit.), p. 407.

[8] It was not by chance that the first writings in defence of the Exercises
had to refute the charge of mystical subjectivism of that kind precisely
in regard to the method of making the Election. (See M.H.S.J., Mon.
Ign. II, *Ex. spir.* (Madrid, 1919), n. 660;661;673;674) The difficulties
that Ignatius had with the Inquisition in Alcala and Salamanca must be
investigated one day and described, not merely as the almost mythologi-
cal-sounding "crosses" such as a "saint" has to bear, but with sober inquiry

controllable mysticism and Illuminism on that account. It will become quite clear that there is no need here. But care must be taken not to contest the thesis itself simply because one fears and wants to avoid something of that kind, on the very practical grounds of experience which has shown the dangers of such things. If one attends calmly and objectively and tries to learn from Ignatius, without claiming to know beforehand what he is permitted to say, one cannot but come to the conclusion that in the Exercises Ignatius candidly assumes that a man has to reckon, as a practical possibility of experience, that God may communicate his will to him. And the content of this will is not simply what can be known by the rational reflection of a believing mind employing general maxims of reason and faith on the one hand and their application to a definite situation that has also been analysed in a similar discursively rational way,[9] on the other.

into the very understandable root of the hesitation on the part of the Inquisition. The question could then be raised whether Ignatius himself in early days, before the serenity which he certainly attained in Paris, did not, in fact, externally very much have the look of an *alumbrado,* and whether perhaps the very reason he later added this or that to the Exercises was to prevent misunderstanding and misuse of the fundamental "mystical" idea of a divine inspiration in the making of the Election.

[9] That does not mean that the contrary of this kind of knowledge which, according to our interpretation of the Exercises, is not in every case sufficient for knowing God's will, is "feeling", "instinct" or something similar, contrary to or apart from the intellect. It is, rather, a thoroughly intellectual operation of the "intellect", in the metaphysical, scholastic sense of the word, in which it is capable of apprehending values. Only it is not cognition of the rationally discursive and conceptually expressible kind but an intellectual knowledge which is ultimately grounded in the simple presence to itself of the intrinsically intelligible subject which in

The proof is not hard to find provided one is not convinced beforehand that Ignatius cannot have said anything of the sort. For Ignatius the Exercises are practical exercises for making a vital decision, the Election. This assertion scarcely calls for further proof. The Election, however, takes place according to Ignatius at one of three times. The first two of these are such as to imply our interpretation, whilst the third is regarded as an expedient if the first two are really or apparently not available. This latter case really is considered the exception not the rule for the normal Christian, for otherwise the first two modes of making the Election would have been put first and would take precedence only *honoris causa,* purely objectively, for the sake of theological systematization, and not because of their practical importance for normal Christian life. Now Ignatius considers the Rules for the Discernment of Spirits to be an essential element of the Exercises, and actually looks upon them as his own special discovery, without which the Exercises would be impossible. But these Rules entirely presuppose our principle and are entirely constructed in order to distinguish from all other impulses those which contain an individual manifestation of God's will and which are not merely promptings from God towards a decision the correctness and conformity of which to God's will has already been established on other grounds. For Ignatius takes it for granted that it is normal to be stirred by different spirits. He thinks "calm" in regard to the various spirits to be a suspi-

---

the very accomplishment of its act has knowledge of itself, without that contrast of knower and known which holds when it is a question of those objects that are known by adverting to a context of sensory perception and imagery *(conversio ad phantasmata).*

cious circumstance.[10] But if the time of "calm" were the normal moment for making the Election, it would not be possible to say that. And if the will of God (in the sense of what God wills), were what can be arrived at by process of reason, then surely the time of calm, when the use of reason is unimpeded by the agitations of the various spirits, would be the normal moment to be desired and aimed at and which would give no cause for suspicion. Furthermore one finds from the Rules for making the Election according to the third mode, that provision is made for returning to the first or at least the second mode. For even in the third mode God is to be requested, himself to move the will of the exercitant and put his will in the soul. And even after the decision has been made in the third manner, the exercitant has to ask God to accept and confirm the choice.[11]

---

[10] See *Ex. spir.* n. 6. That is why the knowledge of these interior movements of the exercitant is much more important for his spiritual director than the knowledge of the exercitant's "own thoughts", that is to say, his deliberate reflections (n.17). (On the notions of "one's own" and "from without", see n.32: what is not free, what does not spring from one's own estimation, is what is not "one's own"). Consequently Ignatius is less concerned in the meditations with what commended itself by clarity and depth of insight than with what brought consolation and desolation (n.62;118).

[11] *Ex. spir.* n. 180;183;188. Compare too what E. Raitz von Frentz (op. cit.p.41) says, "The detailed treatment of the Rules for the Discernment of Spirits shows that Ignatius regards the second time for Election as the usual one". And "regarding the relation of the second... to the third, our authors are unanimous that the one in which God is specially operative is the higher". (Frentz gives references to the old Directories which express this interpretation.) Recently in the same sense, J.Ayerra, S.J. ("San Ignacio de Loyola y la voluntad de Dios" in *Manresa* Nr.106 (Jan./March 1956), pp.71-90, especially pp.88ff.). He shows with many refer-

What meaning can all this have, if one is not to dissolve the words into meaningless trivialities of no further practical significance for the Election, if it is not that Ignatius even in the third kind of choice expects God to guide the decision and then accept it, in a way which, if words are to bear any meaning, cannot, in fact, be identical with our own choice made by ourselves? But in what can this guidance and acceptance consist, supposing it is not identical with the actual rationally decided choice itself, if not in being interiorly moved by the Spirit of God?[12] And what use would all this be if this Spirit of God had nothing to say from the start and in principle, except what is recognizable by rational reflection alone in any case and in any conceivable situation? At most it might then be held that the purpose of the heavenly support given to the decision is to prevent the object of choice from actually being missed, not properly speaking to communicate it, seeing it is there and only needs to be sought. On that supposition the heavenly aid in the Election would only be an *assistentia per se negativa,* to use the scholastic term, the modal qualification of an activity which a man undertakes by his own powers, a pedagogical help for him to attain his own insight, not the communication of a divine will which without such a communication (quite different from support given to an act of cognition), is not to be attained at all.

---

ences to sources, that Ignatius not only had an unmistakable preference for the second mode of Election in his own life, but also recommended its use to others.

[12] For that reason the old Directories expect that a decision made by the third method will be confirmed at least by a subsequent experience of consolation: M. H. S. J., Mon. Ign. II, *Ex. spir.* n. 928; 968; 1161; 1166 ff.

But does such a minimizing interpretation of the thought correspond to Ignatius' intention in what he says? In such a view how could it seriously be said (without glaring contrast between solemnity of phraseology and banality of content), that in these moments of the Election in the Exercises the Creator deals directly with his creature and the creature with its Creator (n. 15)? Why should the thoughts that derive from such spirits be more important for the spiritual director than the exercitant's own thoughts if *ex supposito* these thoughts based on reason and faith were after all what make known the will of God, seeing that this will would in the concrete be fully accessible to them and to them alone (n. 17)? If the knowledge of God's will whether a man is to follow Christ in poverty and reproach only depends on the general invitation issued by the gospel, the man's own willingness and, this willingness being presupposed, his testing by rational analysis of his capacities and endowment whether it is actually the best for him in the concrete circumstances, would one, if one held such a view of what the process of Election is, declare and testify so solemnly to God that one is willing to follow Christ in poverty and reproach "*if* your most sacred Majesty wills to choose and receive me to such a life"? Such words surely refer to a vocation and acceptance which takes place at this very point from God, because it is not regarded as having already happened earlier through general principles of the gospel and through one's own definite predisposition, not even if one's own readiness for such a decision is also included.[13] How could we seriously distinguish be-

---

[13] This is not the place to show that the view here implicitly but clearly expressed by Ignatius does not necessarily contradict the views stressed

tween an indisputable call and grace to spiritual poverty on the one hand and a doubtful grace of real poverty which can be

in recent times by J.Lahitton (*La vocation sacerdotale,* Paris, 1914), and others (cf.Franz Hürth, "Zur Frage nach dem Wesen des Berufes" in *Scholastik* 3, 1928, 94-102; B.van Acken, *Der Priesterberuf,* Trier, 1931; A.Lehmkuhl, "Priesterberuf" in *Linzer Quartalschrift* 67, 1914, pp. 262-297; W.Stockums, "Der theologische Beruf nach den neuesten Entscheidungen" in *Theologie und Glaube* 14, 1922, pp. 193-212). It only needs to be made clear that if "suitability" constitutes vocation (leaving out of account for the moment the call from the Church), then the question recurs, how this aptitude and suitability of the actual individual subject is to be ascertained. Is this aptitude of a definite individual entirely a matter of the knowledge a psychologist, a psychiatrist, a practitioner of mental tests and so on can attain? Or does there not belong to it a complete knowledge of the aptitude in the particular instance, an element that cannot be made fully explicit by reflection and of the kind one possesses with full clarity only if one undertakes that *experiencia* with oneself that Ignatius is concerned with and which is never fully accessible to any purely objective analysis? Such an *experiencia,* of course, occurs in the actual course of living as well as in the Exercises and their deliberate reflection. Even if one is of this opinion one can still say with Lahitton that a heavenly "inspiration" in addition to or apart from this knowledge of aptitude is not necessary for certainty about a vocation. Furthermore Lahitton's principles are after all primarily intended as rules for the ecclesiastical authorities in answering the question whom they are to admit to holy orders and to vows. Now much in the "experiences" which Ignatius requires or expects for finding God's will, is not accessible for an independent investigation by ecclesiastical authority in its capacity as the institution in control even of such "charismatic" knowledge of the will of God, and so the Church cannot pay any regard to these factors, nor can such regard be a duty or criterion for the Church. In her actions as an institution she has her own charisma as a standard (see above, pp. 46 and 60). Besides, no one will doubt that before and since Lahitton, knowledge of vocation has been attained not by rational considerations, principles and analyses only, but by the methods of St.Ignatius, even if less systematically, less consciously and over a longer space of time. Finally, closer examination prayed for?[14] If it is said that one needs for just such real poverty a grace which not everyone receives, then we must reply that the experience that one is receiving this grace (a grace which is clearly not identical with the moral endowment one already possesses which is simply at one's command and only needs closer analysis and appraisal), is in that case precisely the means by which God makes his will known to us. And this will is one which would not be knowable without this experience of grace, which itself is plainly something that belongs to the second mode of making the Election. To be stirred by the various spirits is after all obviously something that appears to Ignatius to be normal for a Christian engaged in the Exercises. Yet on the other hand it is indisputably not to be regarded merely as a mediaeval or antique quasi-mythological representation of the divergent impulses belonging to a human being himself by reason of his own nature. It has to be taken to be a reality different from the human being and his own impulses and yet something that is operative as a psychological movement occurring in consciousness even though it takes its origin outside the consciousness. Now how could we seriously envisage in this sense such an impulsion coming from God, if the purpose of the impulsion were after

of Ignatius' Rules for Election and his Rules for the Discernment of Spirits will presently show that they are concerned precisely with the subject's coming to an experimental knowledge of himself in the congruence of the object of choice with his fundamental religious orientation, and so in an eminent way, with his coming to know his own aptitude for a religious vocation. The theory in Ignatius only explains, therefore, as we shall have to make clear later, why and in what sense this suitability of the subject can and must be regarded as the "will of God". It does not contest the Lahitton theory which in practice is approved by the Church.

[14] *Ex. spir.* n. 98, 16 ("ask for the contrary", not decide on it), 157, 8, 16.

all only something that, as regards its objective content and value, is attainable independently of such a divine motion from without? Such impulses would not in the proper sense make known God's will but only facilitate the recognition of his will. On that view one might still officially maintain their existence but in the long run and seriously one would eventually dissolve the stirrings of these spirits into figurative representations of intrinsically human impulses. For, it will be said, the latter certainly exist, and we experience no others, for everything that we, in fact, experience (unless it is actually a question of possession and so on, someone anxious about orthodoxy will add), can be traced back to these natural, intrinsically human impulses and stirrings, especially nowadays when knowledge of the range, depth and wealth of the subconscious has increased so fundamentally as compared with the past.

If the preceding thesis regarding the meaning of the Election for Ignatius is correctly and attentively understood, there is no need to fear that a door has been thrown open to uncontrolled mysticism. In the first place it is provided for from the start in the meditations that precede the Election, that the objects of the choice must be indifferent or good in themselves and furthermore must remain within the realm of the teaching and practice of our holy mother the hierarchical Church.[15] Consequently a previous guiding knowledge, marking out the domain on principles of the objectively relevant and ecclesiastical kind, is presupposed. To the individual decision in the concrete a condition is assumed: a knowledge of universals. The question need not be raised here why this abstract general knowledge of this

---

[15] *Ex. spir.* n. 170, 351, 353, 361, 365.

realm and domain cannot come into conflict with the real or supposed knowledge of the divine will in the individual instance when this latter after all cannot simply be deduced in its entirety from the former but has its own independent source. The problem need not be discussed here because it is a fundamental topic of general Catholic epistemology, which at many other points has to deal with a pluralism, neither to be denied nor argued out of existence, in the sources and principles of human knowledge, which cannot be subjected to the yoke of a single tyrannical dominating principle (Fideism, Rationalism etc.). At all events in Ignatius' Election this "realm", though the choice cannot be deduced from it, is nevertheless presupposed as a field conditioning possible choice and restricts *a priori* the possibilities of such choice.

This in itself sets up a strong barrier against uncontrolled Illuminism, though with Ignatius it is done, of course, in a way that does not from the start deny, or in practice suppress, what might in an individual case become dangerous, on the grounds that it has already been abused. That way would be appropriate only to the favourite method of the *terribles simplificateurs* in all spheres of human life: A game can only be played with a few balls, therefore they declare that no more balls exist and in any case no more may be used. And secondly, the Election according to the first two modes, and especially the second, is not to be viewed, even in the interpretation we have given, as though quite irrational impulses not susceptible of further justification and of an otherworldly kind were received and distinguished and a decision made in accordance with them alone. Even within this second mode of making the Election and within the stirrings of the spirits, rational reflection can and must develop as an indispensable element in the motion of the spirits. After all, these stirrings do not consist of merely indifferent, blind drives like hunger, thirst and so on. They consist of thoughts, acts of knowing, perception of values, etc.[16] They themselves contain an objective conceptual element, they can be expressed and verified. The experience of consolations and desolations is not the experience of merely physiological states, but of impulsions having a rational structure. They are always also the product of one's own activity of an intellectual kind. They cannot not be so. But that immediately implies that what has to be done in the third mode of making the Election must also take place in the second. The second mode of Election differs from the third not by total disparity but as the larger whole differs from a part which is necessarily contained in the whole even though by itself it does not constitute the whole. And the third mode[17] in its turn is rather to be conceived as the deficient form of the second, a way of making the Election which, as we have already said, aspires to be integrated into the greater, more comprehensive whole.

Viewed in this light, it need not be false in practice to insist that the third occasion and mode of Election should be adhered

[16] We have in mind the case which will have to be analysed in greater detail later, in which the authentic divine consolation of n. 330 is already united with the perception of a really possible object of choice that is accessible to a rational, objective apprehension.

[17] More will be said later about the problem of the third mode of Election and its very possibility, on the assumption that there is such a thing as the first and second methods, not merely as a technique for discovering the same object, but as a means without which what is really in question, namely the actual particular will of God in the individual instance, cannot really be discovered at all.

to, as a defence against facile mysticism and sentimental enthusiasm seeking to avoid the trouble of objective and cautious reflection. For this side alone is accessible to verification by an outside observer and the instruction is, of course, addressed to him, not to the exercitant, who is not forbidden to employ the second occasion and method for making the Election. The spiritual director who is not directly experiencing the stirrings of the spirits, however, though he will strive to have the art of testing these to some degree "in themselves" (according to the report of the exercitant who will try to describe them from the points of view indicated by Ignatius, peace, intensity of influence, darkness and so on), will, nevertheless, despite this art, in which Ignatius himself was skilled and without which one may be a moral theologian but never a spiritual father, chiefly look, in order to discern the spirits, at their effects, that is, the objective justification, reasonableness and so on of the objects towards which these "spirits" seek to guide the choice.

These two grounds, then, afford no basis for rejecting our interpretation of the Ignatian Election by an appeal to reason and good sense and a reference to the dangers of sentimental enthusiasm. Ignatius regards as the normal case of his Election a decision whose content is not simply and solely a deduction from general principles of reason and faith with the help of an analysis of the particular case concerned. Rather is he convinced that in the normal case God in a kind of individual "inspiration" (the nature of which for the moment remains quite an open question), makes known his will, which while falling, of course, within the domain of general revelation, the Church and reason, nevertheless in its concrete particulars can only be known through this supplementary motion from God.

If that is correct and if despite the three different occasions and methods of making the Election one does not want to maintain that these are totally disparate,[18] it must quite definitely be said that the third method must always be regarded as a deficient modality of the one identical kind of Election, the genuine nature of which appears in its pure and fully developed form in the first two. That means that a man has not for his own part the right simply to decide that he will ascertain the will of God exclusively by the third method of Election. This third method is only legitimate if and because God, in fact, to a greater or less degree is silent though I have endeavoured to hear his personal word to me. For his silence is also a way in which he speaks, a complementary form, not the opposite, of utterance. By it God points out for us the modest self-help of "rational reflection". We do not arrogate this to ourselves. And so God opens out to us in this way a domain which was not, in fact, open as a matter of course of itself. It follows from that too, that the three modes of making the Election have one and the same nature and are only distinguished by the differing degrees to which they realize

[18] If what is sought determines by its very nature the way it is discovered, there cannot really, if the matter is properly understood, be specifically different methods of discovering one and the same thing. In our case that may mean that the third kind of Election is not really the discovery of what is also looked for in the second mode, but a sign that the object (a really vital difference for salvation between the possibilities of choice actually open to the exercitant) is not there, although it had been supposed so, and reckoned on. Or it may mean that the third mode of Election is not purely and simply itself but is permeated with elements of the second, (this certainly does not contradict experience), and seeks in accordance with Ignatius' instructions, to develop more and more expressly and clearly into its own complete form, the second mode of Election.

that nature. The first method is the ideal higher limiting case of the second method and the latter itself includes the rationality of the third as one of its own intrinsic elements. The third method is the less perfect mode of the second (and must be so regarded) and itself seeks to rise beyond itself into the second kind of Election.

The object of moral choice that Ignatius is concerned with in the Election is evidently, therefore, of a nature that makes it impossible for it to be apprehended in any other way than by a kind of cognition, a making known, which is in some sense directly due to God himself. We can still leave entirely to one side the more detailed interpretation of this direct character of the manifestation of the divine will. It can be taken as a matter of course not only from the nature of the case but also from the point of view of the Exercises, that the directness or immediacy is not only no *visio beata* but that it is very unambiguously to be distinguished from an actual revelation in the proper sense, as the distinction between the first and second modes of Election itself shows. Yet it must be a kind of knowledge of this will that is distinct from usual kinds, such as, for example, are obtained by the third method of Election, knowledge based on faith and reason drawing on the principles of morality and the analysis of a particular case. God himself "speaks" here in a way that goes beyond those sources of knowledge. Consequently the object about which God "speaks" must itself be different from what those other means of knowing give access to. For otherwise this "making known" of the divine will would ultimately only amount to supporting the other method (the third mode of Election), at least generally in the normal case. For when an object is such that it can be known by some definite mode of cognition (and that *per se*), it is not to be expected that the selfsame object will be known by another mode of cognition specifically different from the first.

Now, of course, it might quite simply be thought that this object is constituted by the fact that God (as the free Lord of mankind) wills some definite thing which in a particular case restricts the range of what in itself is possible for a man and even morally possible from the human point of view, and which as a consequence has to be made known to the man in some special new way. But if one were to think so, or be content with this answer to the question why for Ignatius there is a new mode of knowing in the second method of Election, one would, to retain Ignatius' terminology, be confusing the object of the first kind of Election with that of the second. What does this involve? In the first mode of Election it is certainly a divine revelation that is in question, whether it belongs to public revelation or is a "private revelation". Now if the object of the Election, apart from its quite formal aspect as being the "will of God", were the same in the second as in the first, then according to the principle just laid down, the mode of cognition would in principle have to be the same in the first and second. There could be no specific difference between them. That, however, would mean that fundamentally we would be dealing in the second method of Election with a revelation in the proper sense, whether of a public or private kind. But if this is not the case, as is proved by the very uncertainty which according to Ignatius characterizes the second mode of Election in contradistinction to the first,[19] then the necessity of an utterance by God and one which

---

[19] *Ex. spir.* n.176: *asaz claridad* (much clear light) as opposed to the indubitable certainty of the first mode of Election, n.175. See also n.336.

in some way is direct, cannot simply be sought in the object communicated being a free decree of God himself which can only be known through communication from him. The necessity of the special disclosure of this object must lie in the object itself. And so we seem to be confronted with an inescapable dilemma: The object that is being sought as a moral goal must be comprised in the facts themselves, not consist in an ordinance of God transcending them and freely disposing of them. Yet this moral goal cannot, in fact, be recognized simply by the normal methods of discursive knowledge with the help of the general principles of Christian morals.

If we have not wandered into a blind alley, this dilemma can obviously only be escaped by asking first of all quite formally and abstractly what there can be in the matter itself that is not accessible to the abstractive knowledge of essences as such and yet, nevertheless, can be not only, but also, an object of the divine will. The only answer possible is, something individual in the matter itself which, as something positive (not merely as a limitation and restriction of a universal nature), can in the concrete be an object of the divine will just as much as the universal can.

We can also say, then, that the Election that is ultimately in question here presupposes as its central object, as moral goal willed by God, that element in the matter which cannot be the object of Election according to the third method (to the extent at least in which this method is viewed apart as totally distinct from the second which, of course, in practice it never is completely): the unique and singular as the will of God. How according to Ignatius this, precisely as such and to the extent that it is the content of a divine call, can be known, will be considered in the second part of these reflections. Here we must first of all submit the result so far achieved to theological examination.

Establishing the meaning of the Election and the nature of the method of making it sets the theologian one of those questions of which we spoke at the very beginning of this essay. By the works of those whom God has blessed in the Church, the theologian is not only called upon to elucidate and justify or even perhaps to improve and correct what they say, as though this were merely popularization of the theses of theologians. The question rather is put to him whether he already has at his disposal in his theology the means really to bring explicitly before the mind the concrete experience in question, to make it more exactly comprehensible and to justify it. Or the fact is revealed that his theology would first have to develop through contact with these works and what they say, and allow itself to be corrected by them, before it could do justice to these works and so do them the service which the spontaneous accomplishment of a Christian life should be able to expect from theology.

We are of the opinion that the average theology of the schools has not yet adequately answered the questions which the Exercises put to it in this respect. In regard to the Election there is not yet clearly and explicitly enough a theology of the Exercises capable of bringing before the mind with sufficient precision the concrete ontological and gnoseological presuppositions regarding human living that are tacitly made and put into practice by Ignatius. Something must now be said on this, not in order to fulfil this unaccomplished task, but simply in order to elaborate on it sufficiently to make the meaning and importance of what Ignatius in the Exercises says and practises clear once more in retrospect. Inevitably this involves repeating certain things we have already expressed elsewhere.[20]

We might formulate as follows what has already been said above. Ignatius tacitly presupposes a philosophy of human existence in which a moral decision in its individuality is not merely an instance of general ethical normative principles. There is at least in the domain of moral decision an element which is positively individual and unique, not merely a negative contraction of the general, as in the ancient scholastic Thomistic conception the material individual contracts or limits the specific nature. In the object of the Election there is also, of course, according to Ignatius, a universal essence but its content is not exhausted by this latter. Consequently in regard to that object, ethics cannot entirely consist of a syllogistic deduction in which the major premiss is a general moral principle and the minor premiss is a statement about the relevant situation as the case to which the general principle applies. Anyone, therefore, who intended to compose a theology that would do justice to the fundamental conceptions of the Exercises and vindicate them, would have to show that the actual real concrete constitution of a moral particular is not just the negative limitation of a moral universal to a definite here and now, marking out from the sum-total of what is morally possible and feasible in the actual circumstances a definite item, without this becoming or being more than just a mere instance, a "case" of a certain kind. Such a theological justification of one of the fundamental con-

[20] Cf. K. Rahner, "Zur Frage einer formalen Existentialethik" in *Schriften zur Theologie* II (Einsiedeln, 1955), pp. 227–46. Engl. tr. *Theological Investigations,* Vol. II, ch. 7 (London, 1963) and also pp. 1 ff. above.

ceptions of the Exercises leads in that way, however, to the difficult problem of the relation between universal and singular and to the problem of our knowledge of the concrete individual. The second of these problems would, for that matter, recur even if we held the opposite view. For even with the syllogistic subsumption of the individual case under a general principle, if considered to be a fully adequate method of ascertaining an individual moral decision, one would have to inquire once more how the individual case was known and understood and whether, if the latter is not expressible in general propositions, it is possible to arrive so easily at the minor premiss required in such syllogistically deductive ethics if one is not to end up with purely negative maxims and prohibitions. For with positive precepts and prescriptions the assumption after all is that the situation in question has been fully understood and expressed in the minor premiss of the syllogism. We cannot, however, deal further with this point here.

It would have to be shown, then, that there is, in this sense at least, in the domain of the human being and his personal moral decisions, an individual element which as such, that is, in what it involves over and above the general, has a positive content and originality, fundamentally and absolutely unique. The ontology which would have to be presupposed here would be more elaborately differentiated than it is either in Thomism or Suarezianism. For in the Thomism of the schools at any rate it has not really been worked out that there even is such an individual element. Thomism it is true, in commendable contrast to Suarezianism, recognizes it in the angels, for it recognizes in them positive realities which by nature are not multipliable, cannot exist in a number of specimens. But there is no really fully developed ontological doctrine in Thomism that in a certain manner something of the kind must be true of man and his domain, since he too is mind, freedom, genuine history, *forma in se subsistens*. Yet this self-subsistent form must share the specific individuality of the angels, because it is not completely "immersed" in, communicated to, material space and time which is the principle of numerical multiplicability and repetition of what is identical, as opposed to the individual distinctiveness of a number of singular items. This problem is not clearly perceived in Suarezianism because, though this school considers it must recognize an individuality which is not simply the limitation of the general idea by the pure negativity of matter, it declares this individuality with its full positive content right up to and including the angels, to be multipliable. Consequently, in fact, apart from God, no real individuality which is not just numerical distinctness is recognized. It even holds that everything finite is in principle by that very fact multipliable.

The philosophy postulated by the Exercises would, therefore, have to have finer shades. It would recognize the universal nature and the subsumption of the particular under the general, for in the human sphere there is the common nature of man and general principles of morality with positive content (a universal material value-ethics). Yet it would have to recognize that the universal alone does not determine man, that within it there is and must be the unique, the unrepeatable that belongs to history, what is individual and inexpressible. And all that must be known in a different manner from the norms that are inferred from a universal essence. This philosophy would acknowledge and examine man's different levels and plurality of dimensions and could not tacitly assume that in all human fields precisely the same relation holds good between general and particular. For in the various dimensions that are his, biological, social, historical, mental, man participates in different ways in *ens principium numeri* and in that *unum transcendens quod convertitur cum ente*. It would be metaphysical blindness and rusticity to take the latter for a numerical concept.

Such an ontology would have to show more or less the following. If and to the extent that man as a spiritual person shares in his acts in the subsistence of pure form which is not wholly absorbed by its relation to matter as the principle of multiplicability, he must also in his acts share in that individuality that belongs to the spiritual (to pure form), for this has a positive individuality which is not merely the uniformity of a repeated type, not merely a case of a law. In this line of thought which, after all, is basically good Thomism, it should not be tacitly assumed that the spirit as formal principle of the material component, is the decisive and only valid consideration, and the *in se subsistere* of the *anima intellectiva* a mere supplementary appendix. If the two assertations *(in materia subsistere — in se subsistere)* are dialectically contrapuntal and only in their unity state the distinctive constitution of the human spirit, that too must be taken into consideration when the question is raised with regard to the individuality of man's spiritual acts, whether they have anything in their content of the absolute uniqueness of the angels (and so too of their history), or whether they quite plainly only possess an enumerable individuality of position in a sequence, such as exists in the domain of *ens principium numeri*.

Furthermore it would have to be shown that to the extent that man subsists in his own nature as spirit, his activity is always more than the mere application of a general law (even of morality) to a case in space and time. It has a content which as such, in what makes it what it is and in what makes it imperative, can no longer be totally expressed in propositions that are composed of general concepts. Consequently it cannot be known solely by the methods of abstraction and sense experience, which is always an experience of a material particular, an individual instance. And on the other hand, to the extent that man in his concrete activity as well as in his being as a substance, inheres in matter, what he does is a case and realization of a universal which, as a law formulated in a proposition, determines his action.

It is clear, we hope, from these rapid indications, that there are quite definitely in traditional Thomist teaching, which is better suited to the purpose than Suarezianism, points of contact for developing a doctrine of the singular, particular and individual in human affairs. This could serve as presupposition for what is practised *actu exercito,* spontaneously, in the Exercises without being subjected there to theoretical examination. We cannot pursue the idea further here. Nor can we discuss the desirability of such a philosophy of personal, spiritual individuality, not only from the point of view of the Exercises, but also from wider considerations concerning the fundamental conceptions of Christianity. We cannot here indicate further, either, that such reflections are not only a matter of philosophical niceties but have a definite place in life.

3. The Logic of the Knowledge of Religiously Important Concrete Particulars in Ignatius

The most important practical problem that would follow from such an Ignatian philosophy of the concrete and individual, is the question how this particular that cannot be inferred from general normative principles alone, can be known, especially when it is something imperative that is to be done, when it is the "will of God", his vocation and his grace? It is only at this point too that the full importance of the Exercises for theology is apparent. They are a practical guide to the recognition of precisely this will of God. They are not simply training in the recognition of the general legislative will of God through meditation and deepening of convictions, nor do they merely provide a favourable atmosphere and subjective state conducive to success in ascertaining God's will in the sense of a syllogistically deductive ethics assisted by an analysis of the relevant situation as it stands. They are rather an attempt, especially in the Rules for the Discernment of Spirits, to provide and give practice in a formal, systematical method of discovering this individual will of God. We should even like to risk the assertion that they are actually the first and so far the only detailed attempt at such a systematic method. Of course, right from the earliest tradition of Christian asceticism and mysticism there have been rules for the discernment of spirits.[21] But it is also questionable

---

[21] Cf. for example, H. Rahner, "Zur Geschichte der Lehre des hl. Ignatius von der Unterscheidung der Geister" in F. Wulf, *Ignatius von Loyola* (Würzburg, 1956), pp. 303-41; Hugo Rahner, *Ignatius von Loyola und das geschichtliche Werden seiner Frömmigkeit* (Graz/Salzburg, 1949), pp. 62-86.

whether earlier these were envisaged quite so explicitly as a means of discovering the particular will of God in the sense indicated and of making a decision. Perhaps on the whole one might say that in earlier tradition the recognition of such a will of God was looked upon more or less as the almost miraculous occurrence of a revelation, a heavenly inspiration, or impulse felt as divine independently of any further test. This occurrence being thought to need no further rules for the discernment of spirits, little heed was paid to them. Or else such rules were known and taught, but not recognized and put to use as means of making a correct Election, which has to be made for oneself and in which the correct object of choice has itself to be discovered. That this judgment of the pre-Ignatian tradition cannot be entirely unjust, global as it of course is, and certainly unjust and undiscriminating in regard to various particular phenomena, is shown by the subsequent history of Ignatius' Exercises. Again viewing the matter broadly, they have not encountered very much understanding for their own astonishing originality. That is shown by the perpetually recurrent tendency to look upon the third mode of making the Election as the authentic and normal one. It is betrayed by the meagreness and lack of precision in the commentaries on the Exercises and in other literature on Ignatian asceticism and mysticism. If the earlier tradition had been very explicit and plain on these matters, later times would necessarily have given a clearer echo to the teaching of St. Ignatius. Here it becomes even more evident than in the first part of this essay that theology has not yet in its theoretical considerations caught up with the teaching of the Exercises. Only fragments, obviously, can be offered here on this method of an individual and concrete ethics of the discovery of that particular will of God which cannot fully be resolved into general principles. They will consist of a free movement alternating between the text of the Exercises and theological observations, in which each party by turns questions or answers. All along it is the Rules for the Discernment of Spirits that are discussed, as the actual instruments used in making the Election, that is to say, as the systematic method of the Second Mode of making the Election according to the text of the Spiritual Exercises.

a. The existence of divine influences and the problem of their recognition

The first thing that may be found striking about these Rules is that Ignatius reckons on psychological experiences, arising in consciousness, which originate from God. This happens, too, in such a way that these divine promptings are distinct and can be distinguished from others which also occur and which have a different origin. They are not just traced back to an origin in God in the sense in which ultimately everything that exists and is at work in man is grounded on God's conservation and co-operation, is subject to his providence and, if good and conducive to salvation, can in a special way be attributed to God, to his grace, his providence and so on. To that extent, of course, all moral goodness would be a "divine prompting", a motion excited by a "good spirit". But clearly that is not how Ignatius understands it. He is thinking of God's impulsions, if we distinguished these from those of other "good spirits", as a definite domain not only in contradistinction to evil impulses, but also to the morally good tendencies which originate in a man or are aroused by other human beings.

It is, therefore, a misconstruction of St. Ignatius' teaching to try to start with the assumption that it is only a question whether something is good or bad, that it is fundamentally unimportant how exactly it arose, and that one does not need to rack one's brains whether it comes directly from God or not, for, of course, all that is good comes from God directly or indirectly. Such views and interpretations which can not infrequently be met with in the ordinary average tradition and exposition of the Exercises, are diametrically opposed to the mind of St. Ignatius. For him the whole point is to recognize in the very first place from the source of the impulse whether it is good.[22] The recognition of its moral goodness is, therefore, not the criterion of its divine origin (direct or indirect — this is declared to be all one), but what is sought is a criterion of its divine origin that is independent of the moral evaluation of the object to which the impulse prompts, in order that from recognition of its origin the question of its moral worth as being God's will or not, can be settled.

[22] This proposition is demonstrated by the whole of the Rules for making the Election and the Rules for the Discernment of Spirits. Of course, Ignatius is also aware of the case where it is recognized from the moral evil of the object of an interior impulse that it must originate with the evil spirit. This case, however, only interests Ignatius because by it he recognizes the ungodly origin of a consolation or a desolation, of a motion excited, in which it was *not* possible to recognize this origin from their initial object. For he wants the exercitant to follow back the series of thoughts and impulses which ended up in what was morally bad, and so detect the original quality of the beginning, which could not be unmasked from its own object alone. In other words even in this case Ignatius is seeking a recognition of the moral quality of a movement in the soul independently of the analysis of its object. See on this *Ex. spir.* n. 332-34.

Such a view, however, sets a question to the theologian. Is there in his theology a divine impulse which within the domain in which other good impulses can occur, is so very categorically distinct from them, if the expression be permitted? Is there such a motion from God in his theology as a more or less normal phenomenon, or only in those exceptional cases known as prophetic inspiration, visions and locutions in mysticism, the manifestation and miraculous intervention of God by an exceptional revelation of his will? There is no denying that the theologian of what is average theology nowadays will hesitate doubtfully over such a question. Even a present-day theologian has at heart more or less implicitly or tacitly the impression that everything that God effects (leaving aside the miraculous special cases of the public history of redemption and the like), is brought about by second causes; that these form an uninterrupted chain of causes and effects deriving with orderly regularity from the nature of the causes; that God does not intervene within the causal connections at a distinct place with his own action, separate from the rest; but that he only conserves the whole and guides it by his providence, by which he designed the weave of causes and effects from the beginning, without appearing himself from behind the screen of second causes and their *nexus*. And what according to all theology must be directly attributed to the operation of the Creator — strictly supernatural elevating grace — is surely beyond consciousness and therefore ruled out as a theological interpretation of the "working of grace" of which Ignatius speaks? Certainly it would not remove the difficulty of harmonizing the theology which is customary today with the teaching of Ignatius, if we were only to say that strictly supernatural grace can be unconscious in itself yet that it is possible for effects flowing from it to affect consciousness and that these can be reckoned with. For then the further question would arise whether on this view these effects, precisely as effects of the grace directly educed by God, were distinctly recognizable or not. In the first case the assertion is open to the very scepticism we have just indicated and therefore does not solve the problem. In the second, such an operation of grace is of no use for Ignatius' purpose. For from a phenomenon which is not recognized as grace-effected, he cannot gather whether the impulse can make a valid claim to be a sign of the will of God or not.

There will be no denial, either, that a man of the present day with the attitude to life that comes naturally to him will only with the greatest difficulty be prepared to recognize something that he discovers in his consciousness, as a highly personal influence of God, and to view his states of mind, impulses, his "consolation" and "desolation" as the effect of powers that transcend him.[23] It is much more likely he will think of hormones,

---

[23] One only needs to read the Exercises attentively without preconceptions, taking the words at their face-value. Which of us nowadays would divide as calmly as Ignatius does all thoughts and impulses into two groups, those that are "entirely my own and arise only from my free judgment and will", and those "that come from without", from the good or evil spirit? Astonishment may be felt that Ignatius views everything that occurs in him that is not the expression of his "free judgment", as coming from "outside", as not really belonging to him at all, therefore, as not an expression of his own inner constitution and state. What a dissociation of the sovereignly free person from all that simply takes place in fact, whether it is outside or comes from outside! What a life history is reflected in such a conception, if that man once stood on the brink of suicide through compulsive thoughts! But can we nowadays regard that as a statement of fact about reality itself (see Ex. spir. n. 32)? Can we so easily

effects of the weather, hereditary factors influencing character, repercussions of the unconscious, complexes and innumerable other things than that the idea will occur to him that God, his guardian angel or the devil is at work. He will still admit that all these modes of experience in the inner world of the soul have their religious importance, must be regarded as subject to moral evaluation, and to that extent have something to do with God. But that they could be directly produced by God, will not easily be evident to him today.

This is shown by the very fact that, as has already been pointed out, even the orthodox theologian (leaving exceptional individual cases out of account), is only too easily inclined, in the face of such an attitude to life, to beat a retreat and hasn't any qualms of conscience about it. He will be tempted to regard the idea that an angel or an evil spirit can be the direct originator of a thought, an impulse or a mood, as mediaeval personification of the causes of sudden, unforeseen psychological phenomena

---

admit the bad thought to "come from without" (n. 33)? Can we consider that compulsive thought to be simply suggested by the devil (n. 347; 349)? Can we contrive to dissociate "ourselves" so radically from what is not right, even if it is not an act of our own freedom as we actually know and experience it? On the contrary would we not have misgivings, and theological ones at that, about throwing the blame for all these things so radically on to someone else (the devil)? And from a biblical point of view, should not "I" as "flesh", in which there is nothing that is good, be recognized precisely as the one who (even if not with true freedom), does what Ignatius simply considers to come "from outside"? We shall see presently that one can, without qualms, make excisions here and yet preserve the real kernel of Ignatius' idea of the divine origination of certain experiences "from outside", without on that account attributing to God equally and indiscriminately all that is morally unobjectionable simply because it is good, which is not what Ignatius has in mind.

of which no immediate rational explanation is available. Or he may explain things of that sort as a kind of commonplace and harmless adumbration of what may be experienced in schizophrenia as split personality, feelings of obsession or possession. A thought which has not been rationally controlled from the start, which suddenly occurs and produces a strong impression, is attributed to another person in the typical way in which primitive peoples also do with dreams and so on. Even if one were tempted to propose a facile and hasty compromise in the matter by saying that no doubt there is something of that kind "as well", but that it would be false to attribute everything to it, only an uneasy peace would be reached, at any rate if that were all the solution offered. For we would be obliged to inquire at once how we are to distinguish the two kinds of phenomena which both exist apparently. For Ignatius, of course, the whole point is that we can do this. For him there is no question (as we have already said) merely of distinguishing them by their fruits, effacing the intrinsic differences between the impulses themselves. Consequently he cannot be told that because there are natural and even pathological phenomena of this kind but also others which in fact are produced in a special way by God, it is best to judge by their result: if this is good, that is, if the thing to which the impulse is directed is right, all is well, and it is a matter of indifference exactly how the impulse arose.

Ignatius cannot rest content with such an accommodation of his teaching to "modern" sentiment. It can be accepted only by an interpreter of the Exercises who from the outset limits the process of Election to the method of a syllogistic deductive ethics in which it is clear from the beginning that the problem of God's will is solved by the very fact of ascertaining objectively the actual goodness of the object of choice, which includes, of course, its objective relation to the person in question and his situation. But this view is just not that of Ignatius himself. It is only because many of his interpreters hold such a view that the question we have encountered has not been seen, or people have not been so bold as to see it, in its full acuity.

The first problem that confronts us here could also be formulated as follows. The motion which we are assuming to come from God is either supernatural grace or a miracle and so preternatural, or it is some other created reality. In the first case it is not conscious, according to most theologians. In the second there is presumably no question of it in the normal life of grace. On the third supposition, however, it must be said that any non-miraculous created reality can be produced by other created causes or is at least to be presumed to be so produced until proof of the contrary. How then could one recognize an impulse from God as coming from him, otherwise than in the general sense first of all in which all that is good and conducive to salvation is a gift of God, and then by the fact that it is helpful and good? In this way, however, one arrives at no prompting of God's grace that can fulfil the function in the Election and the recognition of God's will which Ignatius assigns to it in the second method of making the Election and in the Rules for the Discernment of Spirits.

At this point a Thomist theologian might object that these difficulties derive from an assumption which is false, namely that supernatural grace is not conscious. The Thomistic doctrine of the *obiectum formale* of an act supernaturally and entitively elevated by grace, of a formal object of this act which on the one hand as object must be consciously known and on the other is such that it cannot be attained by any natural act, might seem to contradict the assumption from which we started. Consequently, the objection might proceed, we might conceive of conscious and supernatural acts which are directly effected by God and as such come before consciousness. They could, therefore, definitely be taken into consideration as the basis of that consolation which as distinct from non-divine stirrings in the soul, is to provide the foundation for the recognition of the will of God. In this connection it could also be indicated that the doctrine of the gifts of the Holy Spirit as this is commonly taught in the school nowadays, strengthens and clarifies this basic idea. For these gifts are, of course, themselves either immediate promptings of the Spirit of God of the kind referred to, or powers to enable them to be received. What is to be said to this?

In the first place we are not disputing the Thomistic theory of the special formal object, unattainable by an act of the natural order, of a supernaturally elevated act. It even seems to us to be the only correct one. But it cannot be considered the sole and complete solution to our problem here. Not because the theory is disputed. That would not be a reason. For a theoretical doctrine which is disputed as a theory can, of course, actually commend itself by doing greater justice to experience and the teaching of practitioners than views opposed to it. But in our opinion the difference cannot be overlooked between a conscious formal object which is given as the "horizon" of cognition (but not as what is focused) and which for that very reason cannot necessarily stand out in relief against other objects of consciousness, and a content of consciousness which is actually grasped explicitly as an object distinguishable from other individual objects. If this difference is conceded (and it does not seem possible to deny that there is in principle such a difference), we cannot say that the supernatural formal object is more than such an horizon given in a non-explicit and non-conceptualizable manner, the ultimate term and aim, or perspective vanishing-point, of the cognition of objects consciously apprehended in concepts. And this horizon, though known to be present, cannot, nevertheless, by simple introspection be distinguished from the limitless horizon that extends before the human mind through its self-transcending openness in intellect and will to all that is.★

If and because this is so, however, this special way of falling under consciousness that belongs to supernatural acts offers no means of distinguishing them by introspection from other mental acts.[24] But if that is impossible, then this kind of awareness

---

★ *Translator's note:* The word "transcendence" is used in some German philosophy to describe a prime feature of mental activity. The noun is given an active sense. It means "transcending", "rising above and beyond", "exceeding", and the object of these verbs is any particular, anything limited, anything that can be named. Knowing and willing occur in a particular context, but intellect is not restricted to this or that thing known; it goes beyond it, and is actively orientated towards being in general. Freedom derives from this intellectual transcendence, choice is not tied. "Transcendence", therefore, designates the immanent, dynamic orientation of mind or spirit above and beyond itself in endless scope towards being in general and, ultimately, to God.

[24] To the extent that this horizon of supernatural acts, present not as object directly known but only known *of* concomitantly and in a way that cannot be made explicit by reflection, is a simple component of every ordinary supernatural act, and to the extent it is being referred to, precisely to that extent it must be plainly distinguished from natural transcendence as such (the intrinsic dynamic orientation of mind to the totality of being), in order to be known explicitly and in a way that can be categorically formulated. The proviso "to the extent that" which is to be taken as implied in the text, must be noticed, because this is the way the

is of no account as regards the possibility of the discernment of spirits. At least one would have to adduce supplementary criteria as a means of establishing whether the act in question were raised to the supernatural plane and whether as a consequence it fell under consciousness in the particular way that in principle is to be ascribed to such an act. In other words, if being consciously known and being susceptible of being known by deliberate explicit reflection are not the same thing, then the assertion that a certain quality of an act is consciously known (its supernatural quality, for example), is not itself a proof that this quality can be identified by introspective reflection by the mind on the things it is aware of having before it. Yet that is what would be required here. Similarly it will not meet our case to appeal to the gifts of the Holy Spirit. For the question would again have to be put, how and by what criteria we are to distinguish such higher promptings of the Spirit, the existence

objection is viewing the matter. For we will see later that transcendence (in the sense just alluded to) having emerged into awareness, even if it is not perceived explicitly and directly in itself precisely as raised to the supernatural plane, can form the content of the genuinely divine consolation. And this may be so even if the question is left open whether the emergence into consciousness of this transcendence (which is certainly requisite and which distinguishes such a mode of experience from the experiences of everyday), is possibly a natural phenomenon or a supernatural one (mystical, preternatural or supernatural), or even both, according to the level at which the emergence into consciousness occurs. If it is wholly or partly the emergence into consciousness of the soul's supernatural transcendence, through supernatural assistance in a mystical way, then on that basis the points of view once again come under consideration which, outside this wider context, we have just rejected as a solution of our present problem. Consequently the clarification made at the beginning of this note must not be overlooked.

of which we are, of course, not denying, from others. Traditional teaching on the gifts gives no information beyond what is usual and we have already found this not entirely sufficient for our purpose.

Finally it may be said, as is often done, that if God speaks, he will certainly do so in such a way as to make himself known to be the speaker with inescapable certainty. And then reference is made to the prophets and to the conditions regarding the certainty of prophetic inspiration which, as fundamental theology teaches, must be satisfied if the original human recipients of revelation are to have that certainty that their inspiration is from God which we must suppose even the mere hearers of the preaching of the faith to possess. Now it is not to be denied that God can make himself known to the soul in a way that makes the divine origin of this psychological phenomenon indubitable. To deny it *a priori* would only be to declare something impossible that one does not comprehend, or to betray that one has not yet come across such a phenomenon in one's own experience. But we cannot rest content with this expedient which in the present connection is too facile. For the question is precisely whether we can regard prophetic inspiration and revelation belonging to the course of sacred history and which taken as a whole must certainly and necessarily be regarded as miraculous, as a model and example of what is involved here, for after all we are inquiring into a phenomenon that does not exceed the limits of what is normal in a Christian life.[25] Further-

[25] In Ignatian terms: we are discussing the second mode of Election, not the first. The first mode presents the phenomenon that must be described as a miraculous, prophetic experience. Seeing that Ignatius himself, a

more it is, of course, not merely a question of knowing how such a divine influence can be recognized as divine while it lasts, but how this recognition is possible for subsequent reflection and when giving an account of it and for the purposes of apologetics. This too is obviously needed if the occurrence is not to remain like a meteorite in a man's life without entering as a formative power into a genuine relation to the whole of his life.

So even if we do not deny that an experience divine in origin carries its own evidence with it which can never be entirely reduced to another kind of evidence extrinsic to it, because it is sufficient to itself and what belongs to the Spirit "is judged by none", nevertheless our question still remains unanswered. For in general when a rule for the discernment of spirits is to be, and can be, employed, it is to a certain extent *ex definitione* a matter of acquiring certainty about the quality of an occurrence in the soul which comes "from outside". It is precisely the certainty about its own nature intrinsic to the experience itself which is to be checked, made explicit and accounted for. Plain experience shows that this is not superfluous. There are only too many pseudo-mystics who declare that they can have no doubt at all about the divine origin of their interior experiences. So even if one admits that a point is finally reached where subjec-

highly gifted mystic in his later life, as is shown by his observations on his order's right to poverty, preferred the second mode of Election, we are justified in saying that he regarded the first mode of Election as an extraordinary phenomenon which he mentions more out of a certain liking for system than for its practical importance. But then if the second method of making the Election is really to be distinguished from the first, it cannot be of an extraordinary and miraculous character.

tive and objective evidence are no longer distinguishable in the concrete individual case of the actual human being, and where each must stand his own ground with his evidence, it nevertheless remains indispensable in the domain of human society (and in one way or other everything that men experience, do and think belongs to that domain), that an account can be rendered by one to another, especially if attention is claimed from others, or needed. For this can never be done by monotonously describing an experienced certainty as indubitable. Finally is it quite so certain that even the original recipients of revelation did not need the support of, and reference to, external miracle in order to attain explicit, reflex certainty of the heavenly impulsion? Is it quite certain that there really is such a thing as the "intellectual miracle" that takes place in the revelation-experience itself? Does the original recipient of revelation need the reference to the external miracle, verifiable by others, only as a proof to them of his mission? Or does he need it for himself too? It should have become clear that in regard to the kind of heavenly inspirations that Ignatius is thinking of, a reference to an accompanying experience of evidential certitude about their divine origin is of itself insufficient. It would only be the repetition of an assertion that needs to be proved.

b. "Non-conceptual" experience of God

In order to untie this knot of questions, we must turn back again to Ignatius and his Rules for the Discernment of Spirits. What has he himself to say about God's effecting such divine impulses, and about the possibility of recognizing them? Does it turn out that despite all the difficulties we have noted until now, there is a stirring or movement of the mind, the purely divine origin of which is beyond a doubt?

If the question is not to refer to all rules for the Discernment of Spirits (and in view of the objection in principle that we have worked out against the very possibility there would be no real point if it did), the question must be framed more precisely. Is there for Ignatius a fundamental evidence and certainty which is presupposed by the various rules and techniques for the Discernment of Spirits and which performs the same function as the first principles of logic and ontology do for the rest of knowledge and which, distinct from the rules, makes them possible, so that they are the application and regulated putting into practice of this fundamental certitude? The rules would thus represent as it were a supernatural logic and themselves refer back to their own "first principle"? Clearly Ignatius has something of the sort in mind in the Rules for the Discernment of Spirits in the Second Week. Consequently if we may anticipate a little to note this, it is not surprising that this fundamental principle turns up in the second week. For Ignatius it is only in the second week that there is Election properly so called.[26] In the

---

[26] See *Ex. spir.* n. 18. It may be said that Ignatius is almost nervous that the sublime method of the Election should be communicated to those who are capable of initiation into these mysteries of the experience of grace. See on this point Raitz von Frentz, op. cit. pp. 17-20. An attentive reading of Frentz will show that later practice did not fully understand and maintain this Ignatian "discipline of the secret". It was no longer understood that Ignatius when he is thinking of the real Exercises and not simply of pious practices (which can have their use and bring many blessings), assumes in the exercitant a situation in which a decision at the right moment is urgent. Now this presupposes an interior readiness for such a decision, and also a corresponding external situation. A really

first it is only possible to make resolutions which are simply the application of the general rules of Christian morality to one's own life. It is only in the second week, therefore, that the Discernment of Spirits which is necessary for making an Election must appear.

Ignatius speaks of a divine motion in regard to which it is indubitable that it comes from God.[27] The Rules for the Discernment of Spirits or rather the discernment itself as an actual technique for applying a test, does not relate in the proper sense to this kind of divine motion but to other impulses which, since there may be other impulses of heavenly origin and it is very important to recognize these too, are to be tested with the help of this first kind of divine experience as to whether they come from God or not. The first kind is not mentioned as an object to be tested but as the starting-point and criterion of the test.

Here, however, we encounter a new difficulty, for it is not easy to say what Ignatius means by this first kind of divine experience. No injustice is done to the religious genius of the saint, it would seem, if one is of the opinion that he, the man of few words, who had difficulty in expressing himself when communicating his experiences and insights, extremely original as they were and in the way in which he lived them, has here accomplished a masterpiece of brevity but not of clarity. A glance at the commentaries will show that we are not creating obscu-

---

central personal decision is not possible at any given moment, by the very nature of man and the limits of his freedom; it depends on conditions which must be provided for him by a "call" or "summons" (however this actually occurs). Only this summons makes such a decision possible.
[27] *Ex. spir.* n. 330; 336.

rity by reading obscurities into Ignatius at this point. Without further remark one is entitled to judge that they say little on this matter, and what they say is obscure and not very coherent.

We must try to be clear, then, what Ignatius understands by this first kind of divine motion. He characterizes it as *consolación sin causa precedente* (n. 330), *consolación sin causa* (n. 336). Ignatius himself explains the *sin causa* as *sin ningun previo sentimiento o conoscimiento de algun obiecto, por el qual venga la tal consolación mediante sus actos de entendimiento y voluntad* (n. 330) — "without any previous sense or knowledge of any object whereby any such consolation should come by (the soul's) acts of understanding and will". What does this mean?

In the first place it can certainly be said that the concept of the *consolación* is different from that of the object of the consolation. For when it is said (n. 331), that both the good angel and the evil spirit can console *con causa,* there is obviously no question of another series of thoughts preceding "in time" these two experiences of consolation. For why should a created spirit be able to console only in that sense *con causa*? One would have to say that such a spirit can only intervene in an already flowing stream of thoughts and considerations. But then, of course, we would also have to say that only directly on our waking after deep sleep could a created spirit intervene with his influence. For in all other cases a pattern of thought and feeling antecedent in time is necessarily always present, even though it could be more or less appropriate to the purpose ultimately intended by the intervention.

Clearly then here at all events (n. 331) *causa* must mean the objective ground for consolation which is now consciously present and consoling. Nothing else makes real sense of it. But in that case *consolación* itself is to be distinguished from the object that is its motive, the perception or experiencing of a value from the value itself. *Consolación* signifies the inner frame of mind that follows from the object, things that Ignatius designates as *paz, tranquilidad, quietud,* etc. (peace, tranquillity and quiet). The *causa* is simply the consoling object present in the actual occurrence of consolation itself. At most it precedes the consolation in time instead of being merely logically antecedent to it to the extent that by the nature of the case there is normally an interval of time before a person responds to the object and is consoled. Accordingly Ignatius does actually say in n. 330 (at the end, where he expressly qualifies the "object"), that it is the object by which the consolation comes by means of the acts of the understanding and the will. So the object is something from which the understanding and will gradually draw their consolation. So it is naturally a matter of course that in the experience of consolation obtained in this way this object which was already there antecedently to the consoling, most certainly still remains apprehended in the consolation itself.[28]

---

[28] When, therefore, the *versio vulgata* of the Exercises translates: *causam vere praecedere nullam tunc dicimus, quando nec sensibus nec intellectui neque voluntati nostrae quicquam objectum est, quod eiusmodi consolationem causari ex se possit* (we say there is no antecedent cause when no object is present to the senses or the understanding or to our will which of itself could cause consolation of this kind) that is, when the *praevio* of the *versio prima* and the *previo* of the Spanish autograph are omitted, this is not necessarily to be considered as obscuring the meaning. It is more an interpretation expressing with greater rather than less precision the sense really intended by the original. — But if we accept this translation as entirely in accord with the mind of St. Ignatius and take it seriously as it stands, then plainly and simply the consolation without cause is the "con-

From this it is now possible to grasp what is meant by the consolation "without previous cause". What is decisive is not any particular suddenness of the experience but, to put it quite plainly, its absence of object. What this means will have to be explained. There is no *algun obiecto* present, not even in the experience of consolation itself. Now if someone were to intervene at once here with the objection that this involves asserting an objectless, therefore unconscious experience, and this is a

solation without conceptual object". If one adds to this definition what Ignatius had said in the same rule n. 330 in describing this consolation, that is, that in it a human being is "drawn totally into the love of his divine Majesty", then one might also describe this consolation as the consolation without conceptual object in the actual concretely personal, radical love of God. Then the task is to make it clear why such a definition contains no contradiction, that is to say why this radical love of God neither states nor presupposes any "conceptual content" for the experience of consolation. That something of this kind is not be rejected out of hand as nonsense, is shown, to mention merely a random example from the history of the theory of mystical experience, by the teaching of St. Bonaventure according to which here on earth there is an experience of the love of God which occurs without the intellect having any share in it (see K. Rahner, "La doctrine des sens spirituels au moyen-âge, en particulier chez saint Bonaventure" in *R. A. M.* 14 (1933) pp. 263–99, especially 279–89). Of course, if someone identifies by definition without more ado "being the object of a concept for consciousness" and "being known" (of something in a consciousness) we get nowhere here. But to warn and preserve us from making this identification, the simple fact can serve, that there is certainly at least one awareness which is not consciousness of an *object:* the concomitant self-awareness in every act of the mind when it is directed to any object. This awareness is something different in kind, too, from cognition wherein one's own "I" can be conceptually made the focus of a mental act, that is, when I reflect upon the first kind of awareness and express it in concepts and propositions. The question can, therefore, only be whether there can be such a non-con-

contradictio in adjecto, the whole teaching of St. Ignatius would have been quite misunderstood. The absence of object in question is utter receptivity to God, the inexpressible, non-conceptual experience of the love of the God who is raised transcendent above all that is individual, all that can be mentioned and distinguished, of God as God. There is no longer "any object" but the drawing of the whole person, with the very ground of his being, into love, beyond any defined circumscribable object, into the infinity of God as God himself as the *divina majestad: trayéndola toda en amor de la su divina majestad.* This "by drawing totally into the love of his divine *Majesty*" is not a mere addition which even in the description of this consolation as *sin causa precedente* could be omitted or modified (for instance into: by inspiring a good resolution for something definite that is good and holy). It is precisely and unambiguously the positive side of the *sin causa.* It is a question of God and God alone, precisely inasmuch as he is other than any individual object, one might say inasmuch as he is the absolutely transcendent, if this formulation did not have too much the air of prejudging the question of the direction in which a precise theological or philosophical interpretation of the experience in question is to be sought. For Ignatius the decisive stress does not fall, in the description of this genuinely and purely divine consolation, on

ceptual awareness of other realities as well as of one's own "I". If an affirmative answer can be given with regard to God, then, quite independently of the question whether such a mode of experience can exist only within mysticism or also outside it, a "non-conceptual" experience of God in being totally drawn up into his love, is a concept that is conceivable. However, all that must as far as possible be worked out more precisely from Ignatius himself.

precedente, previo.[29] The "precedence" is meant only in the sense that the simple apprehension of an object precedes the actual adoption of a decisive individual attitude of the whole person *(toda)* to it, as we have already indicated. The *sin causa,* therefore, means God himself, alone, not as given in a definite thought conceptually formulated, merely in ideas, not as to some degree "represented" or linked to some other reality, even a religiously important one, such as the particular content of a resolution, a particular object of the Election and so on.

This is made even clearer by the Eighth Rule (n. 336). Wherever there is *proprio discurso,* apprehension of mutual relationships *(habitúdines)* and inferences from concepts and judgments, it is no longer the moment for this truly divine consolation but *eo ipso* it is the subsequent moment in which a man once again is subject to his own impulses and those of other created spirits. For if the objection were to be made that while, of course, in the subsequent period of time there certainly are such discursive concepts and judgments yet these are found also in the time of the *actual consolación* that is directly from God alone, the question would arise how on such a supposition one is expected to be able to distinguish the two times? The first after all has a certain duration too. How would we distinguish the first and second periods of time from one another, if in content they had the same structure? By the first's lying nearer the "sudden occurrence" of the consolation? But how long must the consolation last for it no longer to be close enough to this

---

[29] For that reason n. 331 and 336 simply state *con causa, sin causa,* without these additions, which are not absolutely necessary and must not be mentally added.

sudden occurrence that it had, and for the second period to have already begun? How can it be determined that the first of the conceptual acts with individual objects of thought were caused by God alone but the second by oneself and created spirits? No, we only get a precise meaning (and one of any other kind is none), from the concise indications of the saint, if we see the criterion of discernment between a purely divine consolation and one brought about by created causes neither in the diversity of the causes outside consciousness, which can cause, but cannot provide a means for discriminating between them, nor in the mere "suddenness" and "inexplicability" of the occurrence of the experience, but in the essential disparity of the very structure of the experience itself. On one side there is the pure non-conceptual light of the consolation of the whole human person who is being drawn above and beyond all that can be named into the love of God. On the other there is an instance of being consoled on account of a certain definite limited object.

Although we do not count the history of interpretations of the Spiritual Exercises as part of our theme, we might perhaps add something here, by way of example, on the way Suárez expounded these passages.[30] In the first place it is interesting that Suárez quotes the text of the *versio vulgata* and in the difficulty that he raises over the Second Rule of the Second Week, he obviously fully assumes (n. 39) that what is in question is not the lack of a preceding cause but the absence of an object. For this reason he finds the doctrine hard to explain. He then expresses the opinion that this kind of consolation is given

---

[30] *De religione Soc. Jesu* lib. IX cap. 5 n. 30–41: Opera omnia XVI, 1028–33.

very seldom and only to very holy people. Obviously this scarcely corresponds to the sense of the Exercises. He insists that it is not in itself impossible that there should be an illumination which must be directly caused by God because it occurs without sensible imagery *(phantasma)* and created spirits are not capable of bringing this about (n. 27; 38). Then, however, he says (n. 40), that in these cases too the human intellect does not act without the *cooperatio phantasiae,* as the absence of sensible imagery is extraordinarily rare and miraculous, if indeed it ever occurs, and so he, Suárez, does not care to deal with the matter. Finally the divine consolation that originates directly from God, is recognized, according to Suárez, by being so sublime, so sudden, so much above the normal flow of imagery of the person concerned, and so superior to their degree of mental cultivation, that it is *fere evidens, fere aperte* — almost clear — that the sensible imagery of the person in question cannot be a cause of it and that, therefore, these thoughts must come from God.

Two things are clear at a glance. Suárez has to weaken Ignatius' idea of certainty about the divine origin of the consolation into an "almost certain". And from his explanations it is not at all clear why created spirits could not alter the imagery available (Suárez thinks they can influence it) in such a way that this might explain the sudden and unusual intellectual performance which Suárez takes to be the sign of immediate divine causation. Then there would be no effective criterion of the divine origin of the consolation to be had.

For his own part Suárez is not far from our interpretation. He admits in fact that for Ignatius an experience "without object" is in question. For he puts the difficulty: *si enim nihil objectum est, quid amabitur aut de quo laetabimur?* (If nothing is presented to

the mind, what will be loved, or what will we rejoice about?)
He does not answer this difficulty by asserting that what is in
question is not in the text an absence of object but the absence
of a definite *preceding* cause. This, of course, would at once have
made the whole difficulty appear meaningless from the start.
He does not attempt later, either, to remove the difficulty by such
an interpretation, but tries to demonstrate the divine origin of the
consolation by means of the disproportion between the content of the sensible imagery and the noetic, intellectual element
(n. 40). So for his part he holds that it is in the *content* of the
experience of consolation itself that its origin must appear. Suárez would easily have been able to go further if he had not been
committed to too empiricist a model of the relation between
the intellectuality of a thought and its context of sensible imagery.
For a mode of experience which occurs without sensible imagery or in which at all events the imagery does not correspond
in the usual relation to the thought content, is itself, objectively
speaking, precisely the experience of transcendence. For if we
do not imagine the *species intellectualis* as yet another pictorial
double of the sensible *species* (which would render the *conversio
ad phantasma* superfluous), then what is left when sensible imagery
is absent, can only be the experience of transcendence as such,
and this as a consequence will signify an experience which is
"without object" (non-conceptual), though not without content.[31]

---

[31] Comparison might be made with what we tried to explain in *Geist
und Welt* (Munich, 2nd edition 1957), about the meaning of the intellectual "light" (of the "active intellect", *intellectus agens*) in Aquinas. At
all events Suárez identifies, without basis, "being the content of an awareness" with "being the object of a concept in consciousness". The latter

If our interpretation were seriously disputed, the problem would have to be met, to what extent the suddenness and "absence of cause" (in the commonplace sense of an experience suddenly occurring of which the causes are not understood), can be a criterion of its purely divine origin? Because God alone can work so quickly? Because he in this sense can "go in, and come out" of the soul? But how does Ignatius know this proposition about what is proper to God? Is he suddenly going

(as he rightly stresses) in any more or less normal case builds on a sense image *(phantasma)* or at any rate evokes one as a concomitant phenomenon. Out of this last possibility in fact Suárez tries to construct a case in which, on the one hand, the divine origin is revealed by the disproportion between the sensible factor and the intellectual factor and which nevertheless, on the other hand, does not fall outside the framework of his general metaphysical views on cognition. But it remains more than obscure, how these two cases are to be kept separate, the quite normal act of cognition through sense and intellect, and the other which has a much smaller sense component as its basis. Suárez does not, in fact, dare actually to go so far as to assert it *(fere)*. And that interpretation still contradicts Ignatius' text, which recognizes an absence of object — which is not found in Suárez. It is worthy of note how Suárez stresses the difficulty he finds in this question. He quite candidly admits that certainty about the divine origin of a consolation cannot really be had. The contrary opinion (which to begin with he quotes as that of the Exercises) is, he claims, *"periculis expositum et in rigore falsum, quia sine revelatione non potest haberi haec certitudo* (n. 30) — exposed to dangers and strictly speaking false because this certainty cannot be had without a revelation". He adds that it is to be feared that heretical *alumbrados* may invoke it. Of the Eighth Rule for the Discernment of Spirits of the Second Week he says: *"quorum verborum intelligentiam facilem esse non existimo* (n. 39) ... *et augetur difficultas* ... (ibid.) — I do not consider it easy to understand these words ... the difficulty increases." He says this divine consolation can only with difficulty be recognized for what it is (n. 40). In these straits he has recourse to the expedient of pointing out that if the Holy Spirit beyond his experience and borrowing a dictum of the theologians and one which after all is no dogma and in the sense referred to is anything but clear?[32] That does not sound very likely. For then, after all, the fundamental certitude of the divine origin of this or that consolation, on which all other clarity in the discernment of spirits and all certainty in making the Election depend, would build on a very insecure basis. In regard to the question whether this evident certainty exists, it would be necessary to judge by means of an obscure maxim of an abstract kind, obscure in itself and incapable anyway of providing any real certainty in its application to any particular case.

Finally the unexpectedness, the absence of motive, the surprising character of an experience can no longer nowadays really be a guarantee of its divine origin. We know too much about the subconscious, its sudden eruptions, the astonishing performances of memory operating to a certain extent unconsciously, and of our capacity for logic and combination, as well

---

communicates himself, this communication will certainly prove itself to be that of the Spirit. He stresses that all this is very rare, and this shows that the impression that he does not really know what to make of the doctrine in St. Ignatius, is probably correct. However, he also correctly insists that in the Rules for the Discernment of Spirits, the starting-point for discrimination cannot simply be the content and effect of an impulse in regard to its moral properties, but also the *modus motionis*, its mode, which is either of the sensible order, or purely "interior" and "intellectual". We should only need to say for these: with objective conceptual content and so, as presupposed by this, with sensible imagery; or purely transcendent experience and so without object.

[32] The *versio prima,* of course, says at the end of this Second Rule (n. 330): "*Hoc probat B. Thomas Ia 2ae q. 9 a. 1 et 6, et q. 10 a. 4.*" One only needs to read these articles to be convinced that they are not where Ignatius got his opinion.

as the suddenness (even apart from pathological phenomena) of fancies, moods and so on. Are we to suppose that Ignatius cannot have observed such things, and naïvely claimed that what suddenly appears in the soul can only come from God? If so he would certainly be at bottom an adherent of the Illuminism which sees a sign of the divine origin of a "conversion" in its suddenness. But it is only too well known in the history and psychology of religion to what a degree sudden eruptions and the appearance of new attitudes and sentiments, when characterized by unexpected novelty and a really "revolutionary" effect, may just as well be of natural as of divine origin, or even illusory.

c) Nature and certainty of this experience

How is it, then, that such experiences, of which we believe we have now provisionally discerned the outlines, bear upon them the stamp of divine origin and consequently possess the character of primary, irreducible self-evidence analogous to that of the most general principles of logic and ontology, which makes them fulfil in the domain of the logic of concrete particulars (if we may so describe the domain in which the Rules for making the Election and of the Discernment of Spirits operate), the same function as those general principles do in the abstract domain of logic and ontology? No direct information is given by Ignatius in the Exercises on this, unless we consider the sentence in n. 330 as providing such a reason: "*porque es propio del Criador entrar, salir, hazer moción en ella, trayéndola toda en amor de la su divina majestad* — for it belongs to the Creator to go in and come out and cause a movement in the soul, drawing the soul entirely to the love of his divine Majesty". But then the question arises, what does this mean and how does it give a reason for the exclusively divine origin of the relevant experience? We have already shown that we cannot regard it as an appeal to a theological axiom which would then lend its own very problematic certainty to an experience that suddenly occurs and is recognized as of divine origin by means of the axiom. Besides, it is to be noted that this sentence does not say at all what a quite common interpretation reads into it, and which actually supplies the core of meaning in that customary interpretation. It does not say, strangely enough, that it is a matter of entering and going out "entirely at will". Precisely this freedom to dispose, without reference to conditions in the human being, is not found in the text at all. And what is *hazer moción en ella* to mean, too? Or is once again at this point "at will" to be added as a gloss, meaning, without presupposing any appropriate disposition? But why is that important point not expressly made? Again, how is it known that no preceding cause in this sense is at work? Here too then, the only solution is, that it is not the freedom to enter and depart which is decisive, nor is it in itself the "setting up a movement", even at will, which is the characteristic mark of the purely and indubitably divine motion. It is that coming and going in which God himself as such is given (and nothing else), and that movement in which the soul is "wholly" drawn to the love of God as God (of the divine Majesty). So if there is such an experience carrying with it an intrinsic certitude of its purely divine origin, it cannot consist in a knowledge of God by way of particular concepts in which God is known discursively, by thinking a thought about him. God's presence in it must be of another kind. And this different way of his being involved must *eo ipso* possess intrinsically an irreducibly self-evident self-sufficient character.

If what has been said about the nature of this experience has been clearly grasped, that will plainly be the case.

We have some difficulty in showing why it is so because so far we have avoided transposing, by way of interpretation, the description of this experience into the various possibilities that in principle are conceivable for such a mode of experience. We will presumably not be wrong in thinking that the experience itself can occur on very different levels without prejudice to its identity of nature, which makes all these possibilities a consolation *sin causa,* and permits them to be recognized with certainty as divinely caused. For suppose we begin with the lowest conceivable level of such an experience and interpret in metaphysical, epistemological and theological terms what Ignatius indicates so concisely. This level would be an experience of transcendence, of a certain purity and strength, of course. We do not mean that it would be "natural" in the theological sense. There is nothing that is, in the persons whom Ignatius assumes to be in question.[33] Theologically there is no difficulty in supposing that such an experience of transcendence, attaining a certain definiteness and strength, is always in fact elevated by supernatural grace and is a transcendent activation directed towards the triune God of the beatific vision. Such a transcendence is the synthesis of the intrinsic transcendent ordination of mind to being in general, and of grace which supervenes to mould this natural unlimited receptivity and make of it a dy-

---

[33] On this, see K. Rahner, "Über das Verhältnis von Natur und Gnade" in *Schriften zur Theologie* I (Einsiedeln, 1954), pp. 323–45; Engl. tr. *Theological Investigations,* Vol. I (London, 1961); "Über das Verhältnis des Naturgesetzes zur übernatürlichen Gnadenordnung" in *Orientierung,* 20 (1956), pp. 8–11.

namic orientation towards participation in the life of God himself. Both are, of course, implied in every spiritual act of man which by reason of its moral content in accord with faith is supernaturally elevated by grace. It is clear, too, or can for the sake of brevity be assumed here, that the element of natural intellectuality with its transcendent dynamic relation to being in general, and the supernatural elevation, are not distinguishable from one another merely by introspective reflection. It is also clear that this transcendence of the supernaturally elevated kind which is always involved as the horizon and condition of the very possibility of a mental act directed to a conceptual object belonging to any of the categories, in average acts is only implicit. It is there as a condition of their possibility, as an anticipatory reaching out, as merely a "light" illuminating a conceptual object, not as a conceptual object itself. It is not the object of a concept, not a content of consciousness that can be named and delimited.

It is evident, therefore, that the awareness of this supernatural transcendence, with God as the pure and unlimited term of its endless dynamism, can grow, become more pure and unmixed. The conceptual object which in normal acts is a condition of awareness of this transcendence can also become more transparent, can almost entirely disappear, remain itself unheeded, so that the dynamism itself alone becomes more and more the essential.[34] If this transcendence is present in this way in its purity

[34] By that we do not mean that between transcendence as the necessary condition of any act of the mind, even the most ordinary, and transcendence explicitly experienced, there is only a difference of degree, of greater or less explicitness. The difference can certainly be a difference in kind. The more intensive and "mystical" the experience becomes, and

and as itself the focus of awareness, without being mediated by the conceptual object and so hidden, and if this occurs not only in cognition but also as the pure dynamism of the will in positive affirmation and receptivity, in love that is to say, then we have the lowest stage of what Ignatius is probably referring to, without metaphysical and theological terminology, when he speaks of the consolation *sin causa*.

the more the supernatural elevation of the transcendence exerts its influence (lending a meaning and function which is no longer simply that of making possible the apprehension of objects of knowledge belonging to this world and of God by means of concepts formed from such objects, but designates in contrast to these modes of cognition a directness and independence in the anticipatory reaching out towards God), the clearer it must become that this emergence into awareness of transcendence and of the term to which it tends, discloses a transcendence qualitatively different from the merely concomitant and implicit form. In the text we have intentionally spoken with a certain indefiniteness and almost tentatively, because the question can and should remain open whether there is also a natural emergence into consciousness of this transcendence, either as it is in the merely natural order, or as it is elevated by grace. The phenomena of a non-Christian spirituality and mysticism and also many descriptions of Christian mystical experiences are a warning to be cautious here. The question what precisely is supernatural in a Christian and supernatural mysticism is one that, we think, can still be raised today and which also calls for caution. For is the difference between Christian mysticism and the ordinary knowledge and love of the faithful itself supernatural, or, though still a difference in kind, only one of the natural order of psychology or parapsychology? In the latter case, phenomena that are unusual but natural in themselves are elevated by grace and put to a supernatural use, just as ordinary ones are. It would be difficult to suggest how there could be a middle term between faith here and vision hereafter. Yet mysticism would presumably have to be such a middle term, though difficult to conceive, if its difference from the ordinary life of grace were a supernatural one.

Whether it is possible for such an experience of supernatural transcendence to occur by the conceptual content of the consciousness becoming to a greater or less degree more transparent, or whether it is only possible — as an experience becoming to some extent aware of itself and not as the implicit condition of the possibility of conceptually supernatural knowledge and love — if all awareness of a conceptual object abruptly disappears; whether, that is, to use the terms in which Suárez tries to express this divine consolation, the experience has to be purely intellectual and without any support from the imagination, or whether below this pure intellectuality there is an experience of transcendence which is sufficiently conscious and explicit, and whether such a purely non-conceptual experience of transcendence without imagery is necessarily to be regarded as miraculous or not — these are all questions which we can leave unanswered here, because insight into the character of evident certitude of such an experience, *if* it is present, can be had even so. We can, therefore, leave open in particular the question whether the absence of an object thought or imagined, and consequently of a circumscribed, finite concept when the experience of transcendence occurs and emerges into explicit awareness, can be a natural phenomenon, though perhaps rare in its pure form, or whether it is only possible by a mystical and extraordinary grace of God.

This difference in the extrinsic cause of the one or other phenomenon (if either or both exist) does not affect its inner evident certitude. It is possible to have this certainty about it, as will be shown in a moment, even if it is not known what kind of physical efficient causality produced it. It is to be noted that despite the essentially unlimited scope of this experience of transcendence, its subject in no way has the character of a merely "transcendental subject" in metaphysical abstraction. It concerns, by the very nature of the case, since freedom and love are involved, a concrete person in his innermost centre, as unique, responsible and free. The subjective starting-point is, therefore, clear. It is the act of transcendence of an actual individual subject in the accomplishment of which the concrete human being is engaged with his freedom, individuality and history. But this concrete human being is open and receptive — to the infinity of God himself, and experiences his own anticipatory reaching out to the intellectual, spiritual and supernatural limitlessness of his goal.

It is plainly the case that such an experience bears its own warrant, that regarded purely in itself, it cannot deceive and that in it God himself is present and nothing else at all can be. It is to be noted that it is not a question of a conceptual representation of God, nor of a theorem or a proposition about God constructed out of human concepts which even when they refer to God are of necessity built of the material of limited and earthly ideas and images and with *conversio ad phantasmata*. And in that conceptual description and reference to God there can, of course, be just as much error and misapprehension as there can be in any other judgment or in regard to any other object on which love is freely bestowed. Nor, of course, is an intuitive sight of God what is meant, in the sense of Ontologism or of the *visio beatifica*.

It is an emergence into awareness — we cannot, of course, say "becoming directly the object of the mind", because that would make it the beatific vision — of transcendence as such, and as supernatural, and *in it* of God as the term of this anticipatory reaching out in aspiration. It is the becoming conscious of the transcendence which is the necessary condition of all cognition and presupposed in all certitude; the foundation and ground of all these operations of the mind everywhere and always. But transcendence pure and simple cannot deceive. It has nothing to compete with that might be missed in its aspiration and consent. Pure openness and receptivity is always genuine and can miss nothing because it excludes nothing but includes all. It always refers to the true God because it attributes no law to him that would do violence to what he is and expresses no judgment that is finite and so might falsely circumscribe him. Where the whole of a person's being is poured into this pure movement of receptivity, we have the consolation which cannot deceive because it carries its own evidence with it, presupposes no other, does not stand in contrast to any other that might be preferred to it, and it is the foundation of all truth, certainty and consolation. It has to do with God himself, not with a concept of him. Not that he is seen face to face. But it is not just a conceptual thought of God but an awareness in experience of what alone gives (implicitly and *in actu exercito*) such concepts their real meaning. For a deliberate, reasoned assertion concerning an infinity, when it is always accompanied by a negation, can only be grasped by experiencing the unlimited affirmation which alone makes a negation possible. That is what is experienced here in its purity. Consequently in this transcendence God is present, as coming, not as having come, as the term of this movement that goes beyond, transcends everything and is here experienced as such. And because it is the condition of the possibility of all cognition, it is without error, and is the ultimate certitude. By that it lends the same ultimate certainty and authentic guarantee for us of the term inseparable from it. And since this term is what we call God, we have here the ultimate ground of our knowledge of God.

All that has been said is, of course, not meant merely of an intellectual phenomenon but as freedom and love. But conversely the "consolation" in it is not merely an added concomitant feeling, supplementary to this experience of the free transcendence of the whole mind and spirit. This latter *is* the consolation, because it is freedom itself and the positive taking possession of the spirit raised by grace to the supernatural in its pure being as such a spirit. That is by definition consolation. For that reason Ignatius can speak at this point (and in the last resort only at this point)[35] of peace, joy, tranquillity, as signs

[35] Certainly there is a peace and harmony with oneself which is a sign of the good spirit, even apart from this pure harmony in the depth of one's being which is experienced transcendence. But it is only necessary to inquire how in other cases it is possible to know so precisely, in view of the biblical questioning of our self-assured righteousness, and in view of our experience of possible self-deception, and of our suppression of the truth about ourselves, that one is really "striving intensely to cleanse oneself from one's sins and to climb from good to better in the service of God our Lord" (*Ex. spir.* n. 315; 335). Then too we must inquire what must first be presupposed before we can interpret peace, tranquillity, quiet, courage, strength and so on as workings of the good spirit in us. Then we see at once that the really individual concrete experience of certitude cannot be here but must lie deeper. And it is immediately clear, too, that this real certainty, humanly speaking of a limited and ultimately incommunicable kind which cannot be transformed into a deliberate explicit assertion in conceptual terms, cannot really be certitude in the proper sense regarding our own state of grace. It concerns God, not ourselves, and the experience of transcendence, though occurring through love, is an experience of God's operation in our soul. But it is not in precisely the same sense an experience that we have also accepted this grace of God that we are experiencing; that we have identified ourselves in the innermost centre of our freedom with what we

of the good spirit without falling under suspicion of a dubious spiritual hedonism; and without laying himself open to the query how it is clear that peace, calm and joy are the genuine values, what is right and fitting and good, and why pain, confusion and conflict are not rather the more authentic subjective condition and attitude.

We have intentionally only tried to describe the first stage of this *consolación sin causa*. Of course, it is conceivable in itself and it is taken for granted by Ignatius, that the essence of this experience can assume many varied and higher and profounder forms. We have also said, of course, that the experience is present, though in an extremely implicit, unnoticed way, as a concomitant in every mental and supernatural act, the actual condition of the possibility of cognition and freedom. But though conscious, it is not there known introspectively expressly as such. We have said that obviously there can only be question of the experience of a *consolación sin causa* in the sense of St. Ignatius if, and to the extent that, this fundamental experience of the mind and spirit emerges to some degree explicitly into conscious focus. This emergence into consciousness which again must not be confused with deliberate reflection on it expressed in concepts,[36] can obviously grow in intensity, depth and purity. It need not concern us here how these levels, degrees and per-

are, precisely inasmuch as we are supernaturally transcendent. At all events such an experience, even if it exists, cannot be transformed into a knowledge that a man can expressly state about himself.

[36] Such as for example we are engaged in at the moment by speaking about it. This is done within the frame of the categories just as much as with any other concept, even though it is a case of using concepts to refer to something that is beyond concepts.

haps very marked differences in kind, could be described and distinguished nor when the stage begins that in the strict sense of modern terminology would have to be termed "mystical", infused contemplation and so on. These distinctions are not so important for us here in the search for the fundamental outlines of an Ignatian logic of concrete individual ethics in what Ignatius calls the Occasion and Mode of making the Election, and the Discernment of Spirits. For this so far has only been prepared for by what has been said; it has not yet been expounded.

But we will first support what has been attained, from another angle. There is a commentary by Ignatius himself on the Second and Eighth Rules for the Discernment of Spirits in the Second Week, those to which we have kept on referring. It occurs in one of his letters to Sister Teresa Rejadella. Here is an English translation of the relevant section: "There still remains for us to speak of what we are to think of those things the direct origin of which from God we interiorily perceive, and how we are to use them. It frequently happens that the Lord himself moves our soul and constrains us as it were to this or that action by making our soul wide open. That is to say, he begins to speak within us without any sound of words, he draws up the soul wholly to his love and gives us a sense of himself, so that even if we wished, we could not resist. This interior feeling ... is filled with deep humility, for, of course, it is God's own Spirit that governs in everything. Nevertheless, we can often be deceived in this, for after such a consolation and inner enlightenment, the soul remains behind full of joy; and then the wicked enemy creeps in ...."[37]

[37] *Mon. Ign.* I, 105. See H. Rahner, *Ignatius von Loyola, Briefwechsel mit*

There can be no doubt that this refers to exactly the experience Ignatius has in mind in the above-mentioned Rules. Even the phrases used to describe them are the same. To understand this text, too, we must leave it its full value and have the courage to take it as it stands without well-meaning diminution. On this assumption, we can say that here an experience is in question to which a real and even supreme and irresistible certitude is attributed, not a *fere evidens* as in Suárez. This consolation shows itself to be divine in origin in itself, not by its suddenness and lack of cause. There is not a word about a sudden and unexpected occurrence being the reason why the origin of the experience is attributed to God. A deception is possible in what subsequently occurs in the soul, not in the actual consolation. This consists of a "wordless" experience: without any sound of words.[38]

We can without hesitation replace this by "without concepts", "without particular objects of thought". For unless we are to read it with a sense that is vague and of no account, words and concepts are, in our inner experience, the same thing as objects grasped conceptually and so placed before the mind. This experience lays hold of the soul completely, opens the soul in a way in which it is clearly not generally open, in ordinary or even in reverent and devout knowledge of God. We are,

---

Frauen (Freiburg, 1956), p. 387. (Engl. tr. *Saint Ignatius Loyola — Letters to Women,* New York, Edinburgh - London, 1960).
[38] It would be naïve to suppose that only the sound of words is excluded, but not words themselves, that is to say, objective concepts. For the mystic, words themselves are always a sound of words in comparison with the inexpressible experience which fills him wholly in love of God, who is perceived as present, not merely thought of in concepts and simply signified *intentionaliter* by the concept that represents him.

therefore, dealing with an experience in which the very centre of the spiritual person as such comes into action and expressly so, experienced as such. This actual concrete central experience is identical with a "perception" or "sense". For theological reasons we must exclude an interpretation that would make this a *visio beata immediata* in the doctrinal sense. Nevertheless, it has an immediacy about it that makes it possible and necessary to term it a "perception" or "sense" of God, on account of its clearly experienced difference from other pious sentiments in thought and love. It is consequently clear too that the "immediate" derivation of this consolation from God is inwardly "perceived", and also how and why this is so. The source itself is perceived, the divine origin of the consolation is not merely inferred, as something distinct from the consolation itself, from some marks that the consolation bears. Unless we think of a cognitive power as a kind of peep-show or photographic plate registering indifferently anything presented to it from outside, and provided we understand that the intrinsic structure of the mind, which after all is a reality with a definite nature and is present to itself in consciousness, contributes to determine the character of all possible cognition, even the supernatural, mystical and miraculous, we will be obliged to say that if there is a non-conceptual mode of knowing, it can only be the non-conceptual awareness of transcendence (which certainly exists), or a heightened prolongation of it. On this basis there are no special difficulties in deriving the characteristics that Ignatius ascribes to this experience provided, of course, that the necessary but even in this connection obvious assumptions are made. However, such an exposition would inevitably be a repetition of what has already been said.

It is impossible either to go into further detail here with observations that might also be made about the mysticism of St. Ignatius. Too much would have to be mentioned: the purely intellectual mysticism in his later years to which Lainez testifies (an inquiry into the meaning of this too would be called for), the intellectual side of his mysticism even in earlier periods of his life (for he was never a mere visionary with "photisms" as H. Böhmer makes out, completely misjudging the interior experiences of the saint),[39] and many other things.[40] But above all one characteristic of Ignatian mysticism would have to be worked out which is more directly connected with our theme than, say, the Trinitarian aspect of his mysticism: the finding of God in all things.[41]

This fundamental formula of Ignatian spirituality was doubtless rooted in his mystical experience. It is, in fact, the attempt of the mystic to translate his experience for others and make them share in his grace, as Nadal once said. This finding of God in everything, however, is only the persistent putting into practice of that supernatural concrete logic, of discovering the will of God through the experimental test of consolation. The particular that is met with or that must be chosen, done or undergone, is placed within this pure openness and receptivity of the

[39] H. Böhmer, *Loyola* (Stuttgart), p. 44.

[40] The literature on Ignatius as a mystic is still very scanty indeed. Still worth consulting is: H. Rahner, "Die Vision des heiligen Ignatius in der Kapella von La Storta" in *Z. A. M.* 10 (1935), pp. 17–34; 124–39; 202–20; 265–82. Here too the material can be found to which reference is made in the following lines.

[41] See on this E. Coreth, "In actione contemplativus" in *Z. k. Th.* 76 (1954), pp. 55–82.

consciously experienced transcendence towards God, and kept there. No wonder, then, that everything then becomes transparent in relation to God, that everything is found in God and God in everything, for everything is seen in the ever-open supernatural transcendence founded on the theological virtues and no longer obstructed by the particular object. We would have to note how important it was always for Ignatius in his mysticism that he was able to find God at every moment, when he wished. In other words it was possible for him to preserve that interior openness effected by God, in his dealings with the things of this world. And for that reason he could carry out in everyday life, though, of course, in varying grades of intensity, the "experimental test" of consolation, confronting the particular matter with the utter openness towards God, by the method which he describes as the Method of making the Election. However, all that was only intended as an indication that the theory we have propounded can be fitted harmoniously into the total picture of Ignatius' mysticism.

d) The grace-given experience of transcendence as a criterion for recognizing an individual instance of God's will

That does not yet bring us to the end. On the contrary. Until now we have only really been analysing that fundamental certitude which lies at the root of Ignatius' logic of concrete particulars by which he recognizes the will of God which, over and above the general norms of natural and Christian law, disposes of the individual as such. This will come as a summons to him as the precise individual he is, not simply as the general vocation by which anyone is "drawn wholly into God's love". It constitutes those concrete individual calls in which a definite state of life, a definite, limited, circumscribed object is chosen in an "Election". And this, according to Ignatius, concerns not the end (in relation to which one becomes "open" in this experienced transcendence), but the finite means to it, though in the experience of divine consolation the exercitant had already in some way gone beyond this, in direct relation to God. How does this recognition take place in the Election? How is this divine consolation of transcendence and immediacy inserted as a criterion, in order to arrive at the particular knowledge which cannot be imparted by an ethics of the universal alone? That is the question which still awaits us.

In answer to this question we can do no more here than indicate the fundamental thought by which according to Ignatius the finding of the particular individual will of God is accomplished on the basis of this divinely effected experience. A detailed exegesis of the Rules for the Election and of the Discernment of Spirits is not intended here. The Second Occasion for making the Election consists, according to Ignatius, in one's receiving "much light and knowledge through experiencing consolations and desolations and by experience of discernment of various spirits" (n. 176). As regards this text there should be no doubt in the first place that the two experiences referred to are not simply juxtaposed without connection. The second, concerning the discernment of spirits, is the means of interpreting the first. For these consolations and desolations are not as mere facts a means of recognizing the will of God, but only through their origin being recognized.

The thought therefore is that consolations and desolations interpreted in regard to their origin by means of the Rules for the Discernment of Spirits permit us to know the will of God.

The consolations that come from God also move us to choose and accomplish what God wants of us, while the other consolations or desolations impel us towards or away from what is contrary to God's will. But the following is to be noted. The object of the Election is always a means to God (n. 169), not God himself. Consequently that object is finite and different from the term of the fundamental and divinely-effected consolation which represents the first of all principles of Election. This consolation never therefore has as its direct and genuine object the means, which is the concern of the Election. Secondly the starting-point and ultimate criterion of the consolations themselves and of the Election built on them can only be this really fundamental and certainly divinely-effected consolation.

If these two observations are correct, and yet the Election takes place by means of the consolations, then in this Election of the Second Mode, what is in question must be that by frequently confronting the object of Election with the fundamental consolation, the experimental test is made whether the two phenomena are in harmony, mutually cohere, whether the will to the object of Election under scrutiny leaves intact that pure openness to God in the supernatural experience of transcendence and even supports and augments it or weakens and obscures it; whether a synthesis of these two attitudes, pure receptivity to God (as concretely achieved, not as a theoretical principle and proposition) and the will to this limited finite object of decision produces "peace", "tranquillity", "quiet", so that true gladness and spiritual joy ensue, that is, the joy of pure, free, undistorted transcendence; or whether instead of smoothness, gentleness and sweetness, sharpness, tumult and disturbance arise (n. 335).

On this view it is obvious that the trying out of this synthesis requires a certain time. For, of course, in this kind of Election, in contrast to the First Mode, there is no question of the object of Election itself being revealed directly from above by God.[42] Nor is the judgment bearing on the finite object itself directly inspired by God. Ignatius does not in general reckon on such "mysticism", even if he considers something of the sort to be possible. He has in mind an attempt, undertaken by an individual himself by way of test, at a synthesis of his fundamental innermost attitude, acquired by experience and certainly effected by God, and a definite object proposed from without as a possible matter for a decision of this kind and which had to be scrutinized, and has been scrutinized, in regard to its morality generally (n. 170). Such a confrontation naturally takes time, is really a matter of *experience*. Above all, of course, because it is not merely a matter of a synthesis between the object of the Election and the "object" of the fundamental divine experience. This in itself presents no problem, for the general moral acceptability of the object of decision is already settled. But it is the possibility of synthesizing the subjective accom-

---

[42] As with the First Mode of Election or in general in cases of actual revelation. In these the fundamental central experience of direct relation to God must be assumed to be present and of prime importance. But they might be defined by the fact that in them that experience, by a decisive influence of God, finds concrete expression in the proposition, judgment, precept and so on, of the predicamental order. In contrast to this the *experiencia* of the Second Mode of Election is a "trial", an experimenting at one's own risk and peril, whether and how the central religious experience coheres with such and such limited, predicamental objects. On these matters see also: K. Rahner, *Visionen und Erscheinungen* (Innsbruck, 1952; second edition, Freiburg, 1958).

plishment of the divine experience, as a fundamental religious attitude which must be preserved, with the direction involved in the choice. The subjective elements in both are not at first present so explicitly and perceptibly that it is necessarily evident at first glance when the matter is first put to the test, whether the synthesis is possible.

On careful consideration another observation can be made, and a reason assigned for it through our interpretation of the fundamental process involved in making the Election. Experiences of consolation and desolation of the second degree, those, that is, which do not necessarily come from God but from created causes, angelic, diabolic or human, are probably mostly a combination of the fundamental divine consolation (of a greater or less degree of clarity) and a personal attitude adopted to a created good which is under examination as an object of decision and choice, and arousing consolation or desolation. For in this "time following" (n. 336), the original consolation is still operating, still present, even if no longer in its pure form but overlaid by and combined with impulses that have finite causes and objects. It follows as a corollary that only in this subsequent time is a situation for making the Election really present, if the case of a direct and actual revelation in the strict theological sense envisaged in the First Mode of Election is left out of account. For only here, not in the purely divine consolation, is a finite object, which alone can be a matter of choice in the Election, present, and with it at the same time the principle of selection. For on the supposition that this is not going to consist of general principles of a conceptually formulatable kind alone, the operative principle of choice will be God, or, more precisely, that concrete, unique, intrinsic orientation towards God which constitutes the innermost essence of man, emerging actually into awareness in operation and active accomplishment, and not only in the concepts of deliberate thought about it. So what Ignatius calls *segundo tiempo,* "this second period" (n. 336), is not just a possibility, but *the* possibility, as long as we are still concerned with the Second Mode of Election at all (n. 176). It is the time of *experiencia* in the proper sense, the time of testing and trying out how a hypothetically-settled, particular decision would cohere with the fundamental direction of the spirit of which a conscious awareness has been attained.[43] For usually this fun-

---

[43] In other cases of free choice, too, there is before the actual decision a make-believe of putting oneself into some situation: How would it be if . . . . It is not a case of "thinking it over", that is to say one is not analysing the object of possible choice in factual, rational considerations. One is trying out in a sort of make-believe or even play-acting experiment, whether one can discover in oneself in regard to the object of choice a certain global "connaturality" (to use Aquinas' term: 2a 2ae q. 1 a. 4 ad 3; q. 45 a. 2; cf. Denzinger 2324), which is not susceptible of further explicit analysis. Elsewhere in the Exercises Ignatius mentions this preliminary getting attuned to, and putting oneself into, a certain situation. See, for example, *Ex. spir.* 185–87 and 339–41. It is remarkable to find it precisely in the Third Mode of making the Election. It shows that Ignatius' rational method of making the Election when more intense divine consolation is lacking, is not a purely discursive one after all. It is always a matter of a person's putting himself into a certain situation, possibly with the help of the device of putting himself in someone else's place, in order to mobilize the actual real centre of his own nature in relation to the situation, so as to bring into full awareness how the person he really is (which may be hidden from him), reacts to some possible object of choice. Viewed from this angle, the Method of Election of the Second Mode in Ignatius is only the sublime case of an occurrence that is found elsewhere too. For here it really is the innermost centre of the person that is mobilized: his pure openness to God in his own way as precisely this individual human being in a supernatural dynamism. And

---

damental dynamic orientation is only there as the implied condition of the possibility of being occupied with the individual realities of life and the world around, or else it is known by deliberate reflection and has become the object of conceptual thought and general propositions.

From this angle we should have now to indicate how Ignatius describes the *experiencias* which supply the signs for recognizing whether the object of Election is in accord with the purely divine experience or not and consequently to be considered an object that has come from God or has been insinuated from below. However, this description will not be undertaken in any more detail. We should only like to emphasize once more that these signs do not consist in an objective judgment of the object of decision by objective principles relevant to the object in question itself. To be sure Ignatius knows of this method too, not only in the Third Mode of Election (n. 177–79; 181), but also in the process of making the Election according to the Second Method. For in the reflection on how the hypothetical object of choice affects the innermost fundamental attitude actualized in the purely divine consolation, it is also possible to consider whether through the dynamic influence exerted already on the exercitant by such a possible choice, something in fact evil is gradually becoming the purpose of the impulsion (cf. n. 333). But the real signs of the congruence and coherence of the two factors which are confronted with one another in the Second Mode of Election are, after all, essentially of a different kind: peace, joy, tran-

what he confronts therewith is not just anything but something that is both important for salvation and that has already passed the scrutiny of abstract morality and ecclesiastical acceptability (n. 170).

quillity, quiet, gladness, interior joy, warmth and favour.[44] It is precisely from them that it is to be recognized whether the object in question in the Election is good or not. But all these signs are only aspects of what we have called congruence between the divine consolation and the prospective putting of oneself in the situation of having chosen a certain object, or between the fundamental attitude and the particular decision. And this congruence is to be understood as experienced by the exercitant, not as estimated by deliberate evaluation with the object as starting-point. It is, however, impossible here to go into further detail on this.

Another quite important point can be made on that basis. We said earlier that Ignatius' whole system of finding the particular will of God in the concrete would collapse if we were to maintain that it did not matter whether the impulses came from God and his angels or from a good natural disposition or, on the contrary, from concupiscence or from the evil spirit; that it is not important to distinguish them by their origin which is, after all, impossible; but that it is sufficient to diagnose their moral quality, for that is all that matters and the other is impossible in practice. We pointed out that this amounts to rejecting the essence of Ignatius' logic of making the Election. For him the whole sense of his precepts for making the Election depends on the moral value of the relevant object of choice being recognized from its being inspired by God or the devil. The discernment of its origin is therefore the radical condition

---

[44] *verdadera alegría y gozo spiritual*: 329; *paz, tranquilidad y quietud*: 333; *suavidad y gozo spiritual*: 334; *dulce, leve y suavemente con silencio*: 335; *caliente y favorescida*: 336.

of the possibility of distinguishing its moral value. Consequently the two cannot be identified and the knowledge of the second cannot be arrived at, in Ignatius' view, without its logical foundation, knowledge of its origin.

We can now make this statement rather more precise. Everything depends on our recognizing the purely divine consolation as being of divine origin. It is the real and ultimately sole principle of the remainder of the Discernment of Spirits and consequently of the process of making the Election. It follows that it need not be clear whether other consolations when genuine, that is, morally good, come from the good disposition of nature, the good angel or from God, or whether the false consolations or desolations owe their origin to the concupiscence of human nature or to the evil spirit. That is not of decisive importance. Even if we are rather more cautious in this matter than Ignatius was and regard much of the old tradition (which was apt very readily to see good and evil spirits at work), as something in the nature of mythological personification, that has no importance for the essence and permanent value of Ignatius' logic of making the Election. The genuinely fundamental divine consolation is not in any way "mythological", in the way Ignatius understood it and as we have attempted to explain it. Its entire origin from God alone is just as comprehensible and indubitable today as in Ignatius' time.

This raises a question that has already been touched upon implicitly but which deserves explicit treatment too. For Ignatius the really normal Occasion and Mode for making the Election is the second, because there is a particular object of individual choice and this cannot be recognized by discursive conceptual thought alone. What about those people then who are not capable of making the Exercises? After all Ignatius says there are such people. Does a will of God of a quite different type suddenly appear in the Third Occasion of making the Election? In other words, is there always and everywhere, whether from the point of view of subject or object, only this particular and individual will of God, which, of course, includes his general will regarding essential natures but is not exhausted by it and goes beyond it? It would surely have to be so if the theory that has been expounded were accepted. But how is that tenable, seeing that most human beings in their choices do not seem to trouble about such a thing and could not, even if they wanted to?

To elucidate this question we must remember in the first place that it is quite an ordinary thing for people not to notice some moral aspects of their actions, so that their decisions cannot take them into account. The same thing happens with regard to the essential features of the reality they have to deal with. So it is not surprising if, in fact, a good deal in the prescriptions of individual ethics escapes people, though in themselves they apply. Furthermore it must not be forgotten that there are very many objects of choice which despite their material diversity are not formally disparate, that is, in relation to their congruence with the fundamental concrete tendency of an individual person as actualized in the experience of "consolation". In simple terms there are very many things which for all the differences between them are indistinguishable as means to eternal salvation, at least in any discernible way. It goes without saying, therefore, that such things are not to be subjected to the method of Election which we have described. Very likely there are more things which are indifferent in this sense than is commonly thought. For however many material factors of that kind in moral decisions and behaviour enter into moral action and contribute to constitute it, there is a very great range of possibilities in the way this material, with its considerable ethical plasticity, can be taken and shaped and envisaged. Consequently from many points of view and in very many cases it does not matter so much what one does and chooses but how one handles what one has by whatever method decided upon and what one makes of it oneself.

It may be said too that nearly everyone in grave decisions makes a choice more or less exactly in the way Ignatius conceives it, just as the man in the street uses logic without ever having studied it, and yet it remains useful to draw inferences by means of logic that one has studied. In such decisions a man thinks things over for a long time. Consequently in every case he will probably make his decisions through a fundamental global awareness of himself actually present and making itself felt in him during this space of time, and through a feeling of the harmony or disharmony of the object of choice with this fundamental feeling he has about himself. He will not only nor ultimately make his decision by a rational analysis but by whether he feels that something "suits him" or not. And this feeling will be judged by whether the matter pleases, delights, brings peace and satisfaction. There is much significance in this use of the word peace to describe what is found in a right decision.

The difference between Ignatius' logic of concrete particulars and that of daily life does not, then, lie in the formal structure of each, but in their application to a particular range of objects. With Ignatius it is a question of recognizing the harmony between the object of choice and a person's precise individual mode of religious life. But we can also suppose that the faithful who have never heard of St. Ignatius' instructions nevertheless instinctively make their religious decisions by their everyday religious logic in essentially the same way as Ignatius provides for. For example, the actual way a vocation to the religious life is discovered will not be in contradiction to it. In an individual case who can state fully the actual concrete grounds of the actual individual vocation, so that it would be possible to say that these and these alone were what really decided the matter? Yet the person who is certain of his vocation has a real certainty which cannot be fully reconstructed out of rationally analysable grounds. If, nevertheless, someone wanted and had to indicate more precisely what this certainty was like and how it arises, could they say anything very different from what Ignatius says? Is his teaching not the elaborated technique, worked out into its essentials, of what the faithful do by and large every day but with a greater risk of gross failures?

Nor does Ignatius envisage in the Third Mode of making the Election anything fundamentally different as object of choice from what, according to our interpretation, the object of an Election must always in principle be for Ignatius. For we can at once reckon with the possibility that in cases where the stirrings of the spirits such as characterize the first and second occasions for making the Election are lacking in regard to some object of choice, this is simply a sign that this object of Election and its contrary are indifferent as regards an individual religious decision, though the object itself may not seem so. For that reason it does not and cannot enter into consideration for an Election made by the second method through the *experiencia* of divine consolation. That is not surprising and at the same time it in no way disproves the thesis that every individually important question can be clarified only by this method of the Second Mode of Election.

Besides, the situation of someone who must fend for himself with his reasonings and reflections (and yet, as Ignatius holds, is striving to return to the second mode of Election), is not one that he chooses of his own accord. The exercitant and his spiritual director have, of course, seriously attempted the second mode (n. 6 etc.). The third is only employed if and because the second is not available: "If the Election does not proceed on the first or second occasion, there follow as regards the third . . .' (n. 178). The third mode, therefore, is not selected because a man is free to pick his method of Election at will, but because God authorizes him to use it by relegating him to that position. The experience of not receiving consolation is itself a factor in the Election made according to the third mode. It may show the actual indifference of the object of Election in this particular instance, so that choice may be made by purely ratiocinative methods. Or this silence of God may itself be an answer, manifesting his will for the exercitant to remain in the darkness of uncertainty, of the provisional, of unfinished experiment. Or else perhaps in actual fact the process of the second mode is occurring but in a less explicit form, at a time which the exercitant interpretes as "calm". For, of course, Ignatius calls this period *tiempo tranquilo*, "time of calm" (n. 177). It will hardly be disputed that he was not overlooking that the *tranquilidad y quietud,* "calm and quiet" (n. 333), is also to be regarded as a sign of motion by the good spirit. That serene, joyous and harmonious lucidity in which there can alone be any hope of finding the correct solution in individually important affairs, may also be a fruit of the spirit. It may be that delicate receptivity to God, which a man does not notice at all, and so he thinks he has found the right solution by pondering and calculating acutely and lucidly, pencil in hand, without being moved by any spirits at all. One cannot, therefore, say that the existence of a third mode of Election for Ignatius, who looks upon it essentially as subsidiary or as a factor in the second mode of Election, disavows the thesis that what is individually, vitally and above all religiously and morally important can in principle only be discovered by the logic which Ignatius makes explicit and brings to our attention in the Rules for the Election and in the Rules for the Discernment of Spirits.

In these last sections we have to all appearance made more assertions than we have propounded questions. But even so the intention has really only been to permit the Exercises to put questions to theology. Especially the question whether it is adequately equipped to expound and explain the religious activities that are described and above all prescribed in the Exercises. If the reader surveys once again the second part of this essay he will probably rather incline to the opinion that there is still much needed before theology can assimilate and bring explicitly forward for reflection this logic of the discovering of God's will. It is not the logic of a deductive ethics of general principles, though this too is necessary and the Exercises take its existence for granted. It is a logic of concrete individual knowledge which can only be attained in the actual accomplishment of concrete cognition itself, in this instance knowledge of the particular will of God addressed to the individual as such.[45]

---

[45] As such! Need we repeat that everything general and quidditative in a concrete reality in fact or in act is, on principle, the object of rational knowledge in accord with the general principles of natural law, logic and the canons of faith, with the help of rational analysis of the relevant situation, in which right action is only possible if it is in accordance with these principles.

Are we not entitled to say that in the Exercises Ignatius wrote lines which have not yet been transformed into the necessary pages in treatises of moral theology? It is no answer to allege that such pages would only belong to ascetical literature. For in books of practical asceticism addressed to the faithful at large there should, after all, only be found what would not be out of place in ascetical theology, though no doubt in the latter it would be on a higher level of abstraction. And ascetical theology can only be conceived as an integral part of moral theology. If such pages are lacking to it and yet are only found in very faulty form in practical ascetical literature, it is not to be denied that the theology of the schools still can and ought to go to school to this master of life. Everything that has been said here should only be understood as drawing attention to a modest question, in a matter of importance, addressed to theology by a holy teacher of the Christian view of life and of its practice. He is still far from having spoken his last word in the Church in such a way that it has been fully understood and so ceased to be really his own.

QUAESTIONES DISPUTATAE

KARL RAHNER
INSPIRATION IN THE BIBLE

Karl Rahner, professor of dogmatic theology at Innsbruck, examines the question of scriptural inspiration with the conviction that the whole issue could benefit by being completely re-thought. He suggests, therefore, an entirely new approach to the mystery, in which the Scriptures are seen primarily as an essential and constitutive element of the Apostolic Church, and their inspiration simply as part of the activity of God in establishing the Church as the guardian of the deposit of faith. The study is intentionally provocative, but no one conservant with the subject of inspiration can fail to find here food for thought and reflection.

HERDER AND HERDER

QUAESTIONES DISPUTATAE

KARL RAHNER

ON THE THEOLOGY OF DEATH

The author treats of the nature of the Christian's death from the
theological point of view and on the special mode of death called
martyrdom. He is concerned with opening up new perspectives in
older problems, striving to formulate new and more fruitful concepts
for the penetration of one of the most important dimensions of Christian
belief and experience. Writing with the great care necessary in theological discussion and abstaining from technical terminology and
"jargon", he conveys a sense of the intellectual urgency and the
exploratory nature of the enquiry. This book forms part of a new
series of short treatises entitled *Quaestiones Disputatae* in which some of
the more urgent "open" questions of the Christian faith are discussed
by eminent Catholic writers.

HERDER AND HERDER

QUAESTIONES DISPUTATAE

KARL RAHNER
THE CHURCH AND THE SACRAMENTS

The connection between the Church and the sacraments is not very clear in the minds of the faithful or even among theologians. The Church dispenses the sacraments, it is said, which are the means of grace for the salvation of the individual. But the relationship between Church and sacraments is often treated almost as if God might have entrusted their administration to some other institution.

Karl Rahner sets the question in a wholly new framework by seeing the Church as the enduring presence of Christ in the world and thus as truly the fundamental sacrament, the source of all the sacraments. He emphasizes their importance as signs; they are causes of grace precisely because they are signs and symbols of God's presence. Just as the sacraments are acts fundamentally expressive of the nature of the Church, so the Church experiencing her own nature by fulfilling it, recognizes that certain acts flowing from this nature are sacraments.

This approach enables the author to show the difference between the *opus operatum* and the *opus operantis* not to be as radical as mediocre theology often suggests. He is also able to circumvent the historical difficulty of proving the particular institution by Christ of certain sacraments such as matrimony, holy orders, extreme unction and confirmation. The dispute between Catholics and Protestants over the number of sacraments actually instituted by Christ in Holy Scripture thus becomes a relatively subordinate problem. The book at once provides a new schema for ecumenical discussion, and is bound to provoke much rethinking of traditional Catholic and Protestant statements concerning the sacraments, and will contribute to the deepening of the sacramental lives of many.

HERDER AND HERDER

QUAESTIONES DISPUTATAE

KARL RAHNER
VISIONS AND PROPHECIES

What does the Church mean when she recognizes private revelations and visions as credible? Which is the point at which God affects the soul? What are the criteria for the discernment of genuine prophecies? Karl Rahner's concern is the theological and psychological significance of phenomena which, despite the Church's care in establishing their authentic character, have been left too often and too readily to human credulity. The danger of error, he suggests, is greater in credulity than scepticism. He offers what is in effect a general theory that "genuine" private revelations are to be judged as an overflow into the sensibility of a primarily spiritual impulse and, consequently, combine "subjective" with "objective" elements. Mystical visions deserve the respect due to the spiritual life of sane and devout people, but the supernatural agency is not to be presupposed but must be proved. As regards prophetic visions, their only absolute criterion is a miracle performed in connection with the prophecy so as to be understood as its confirmation. Expressing reservations on the alleged miracles of Fátima and La Salette Father Rahner shows that divine prophecies cannot be intended to restrict human liberty and, in post-apostolic times, must fit into the framework of scriptural prophecy. This is a bold application of theological principles to a subject beset by devotional prejudices and preconceptions.

HERDER AND HERDER